schooled

schooled

A Love Letter to
the Exhausting, Infuriating,
Occasionally Excruciating
Yet Somehow Completely Wonderful
Profession of Teaching

stephanie jankowski

Founder of
When Crazy Meets Exhaustion

PAGE STREET
PUBLISHING CO.

PAGE STREET
PUBLISHING CO.

Copyright © 2019 Stephanie Jankowski

First published in 2019 by
Page Street Publishing Co.
27 Congress Street, Suite 105
Salem, MA 01970
www.pagestreetpublishing.com

Distributed by Macmillan, sales in Canada by The Canadian Manda Group.

23   22   21   20   19   1   2   3   4   5

ISBN-13: 978-1-62414-876-7
ISBN-10: 1-62414-876-X

Library of Congress Control Number: 2019932490

Book design by Kylie Alexander for Page Street Publishing Co.
Cover illustration by Mina Price

Printed and bound in the United States

For my VHS family

Table of Contents

Introduction

The truth is, I never planned on writing this book. Sure, publishing my word babies has always been a pipe dream, a bucket list item, but so has being invited to Tina Fey's house for drinks, so there's that. Without getting all sappy, I believe this book picked me. What's weird is that's exactly how I feel about teaching: The profession picked me, not the other way around.

Schooled is the marriage of kismet and two decades steeped in education.

I started teaching straight out of college, which meant I was 22 years old while many of my students were 18. And yes, my first year was the cluster you're imagining. I punctuated nearly every school day with a good cry on the way home. But I stuck it out in the Pennsylvania public school system, where I worked as a high school English teacher, SAT preparation instructor and writing tutor before transitioning to the world of online learning, which is where I've been for the last ten years. Teaching remotely has given me opportunities I don't know I would've otherwise had, most notably, being able to stay home with my kids. But this is a book about education, so let's focus, people. Virtual networking opened doors for me to write for educational websites, such as We Are Teachers, various colleges and universities and ed-tech companies. Somewhere in there I started a blog, When Crazy Meets Exhaustion, which is probably blocked from your workplace because of the inadvertent inclusion of the word "sex" in its URL. Ooopsie. The blog birthed a Facebook page where today, more than 60,000 pals and educators laugh and learn, two things I think belong together.

Look, I know there's a lot wrong in our schools today, and many of us have been tempted to throw up deuces and run away. But ohmygoodness, there's also so much about teaching that's right and good and amazing. The very soul of our profession is helping kids believe in themselves; is there a better feeling than watching a child succeed? Dear educators, the work we do matters. *It matters*. I know it doesn't always feel that way, but I promise you, teachers make an important difference. Bump into a former student at a baseball game or at the grocery store and watch her face light up when she sees you. Reread the thank-you notes you keep in the treasure box that is your bottom desk drawer. Remember the time that graduate came back to school just to tell you how much your class prepared him for college. I get it, you guys. Teaching is the best and worst profession all wrapped up in a job that resembles a lifestyle more than a career choice, and if you feel that in your bones, then you are my people.

All teachers have enough material to fill their own book. Their pages, much like mine, would be wrought with stories of the otherworldly joy, unfathomable anguish and the laugh-'til-you-pee funnies our profession doles out in spades. This book is dedicated to those teachers and the hard stuff we do every damn day.

Thank you for reading.

xo,

Stephanie Jankowski

part I

Back to School

Teacher Truth

Until there's a college course that throws us into a sweltering classroom with 30 students, enough materials for half of them and no time to pee, no one will truly be prepared to enter the profession of teaching.

When You're a 22-Year-Old Teacher and Your Students Are 18

H all Duty, 2004.

Because my colleague had to cover another class, I was canvassing the halls solo that day. It was eerily quiet, the usual suspects nowhere to be found. I'd grown accustomed to multiple trips around the building—front to back, up and down the steps—and learned that changing into comfortable sneakers was a necessity. Heels stashed under my desk back in the classroom, I was business on top and Nike runners on the bottom as I walked the halls of our high school that day.

In retrospect, it made sense: a young-looking female, tennis shoes, hair pulled back in a low ponytail. I should've seen it coming.

Rather, I should've seen *her* coming.

Passing the copy center, I continued down the long empty corridor, removed from the steady lineup of classroom doors.

As I rounded the corner leading to the gym's back entrance, the most remote part of the building, I heard a quick shuffling behind me. She grabbed me by the arm just above the elbow, spinning me around to face her. Stunned, I couldn't find words; there was no time. Her hot breath flooded my face, our noses mere inches apart. "What do you think you're doing? Get back to class!"

Sighing loudly, I rolled my eyes. "Yeah, hi. Barbara? We've been through this. I work here. I'm a first-year teacher."

This was the eleventh time our school nurse had intercepted me in the hall with accusations of cutting class. I'd run out of fucks somewhere around our third confrontation.

Barbara released her death grip and took a few steps back, studying me. Her eyes widened in surprised amusement to find me on the receiving end of her mistake once again. "I just keep thinking you're one of the students!" I fought the urge to roundhouse her. This level of stupidity was ridiculous. Not to mention the fact that she put her hands on me—again. She's lucky I wasn't one of the students, because I'd seen enough of them throw down with one another in those very hallways and one even try to fight our principal. Either our nurse was unaware of her handsy repercussions or she just didn't care. I was leaning toward the latter.

So many bizarre and blatantly inappropriate things happened during my first year of teaching, most of them simply because I was a young woman. Beginning a career at the age of 22 is a daunting task for anyone, but when your subordinates are only a couple years younger, and when those subordinates are actually juniors and seniors in your

English class, situation and circumstance are complicated in a way I never learned about in college.

Like the day my students were working in pods. To accommodate the desks, I had to move a cluster of them close to the door. The move was against my better judgment, as I was all too familiar with the risks of desk-to-door proximity. No teacher in America can compete with the temptation that is The Hallway. I've seen students break their necks for just a quick peek into the enticing abyss outside the classroom. Voices, footsteps, the bang of a locker—teachers don't stand a chance. And if someone knocks on the door? *Mayhem*.

Unfortunately, I had no choice that day; the pods were a necessary evil. I ran interference as best I could by physically standing between the students and the door, but because it was approximately 105°F that September, the door and windows had to remain open if there was any chance of survival.

P.S. Ms. DeVos, please do something useful like equipping schools all over America with air-conditioning. Or resigning. Thank you.

Moving on.

One of the usual hall wanderers was in full effect that day. I didn't realize it, but he was lingering just outside my class-room and any time I stood in front of the door, specifically when I bent over a desk to help students, this young man was . . . how do I put this delicately?

He simulated . . . no.

He pretended to . . . not quite right.

He . . . okay, fine. I'm just gonna say it.

He air-humped me. And I was completely oblivious, chatting up students about the author's purpose in the text. Not until one of my female students quietly motioned toward the door did I catch him in the act.

Lesson #80,023 we do not learn in college: the proper way to handle a student simulating a sex act on us.

I'm generally quick-witted and rely on humor to diffuse uncomfortable situations (shoulda seen me at my grandmother's funeral! I was a riot, I tell ya!), but even I couldn't find the funny in a student sexually harassing me. I was livid! My anger didn't stem from the fact that I was the teacher; I was a *person*, one who had shown those kids nothing but kindness and respect, and this is how they repaid me? Many of my students were only a few years younger than me, making it super difficult to establish my authority in the first place. I was quickly meeting my limit for bullshit. Between the school nurse's antics and parents not realizing (or believing!) I was their kids' teacher, and now this student's terrible, horrible, no good, very bad decision, I was ready to snap.

I stood in the doorway, watching the air humper book it down the hallway, and said nothing. There was no joke appropriate for the situation, and it wasn't just me who felt it. The whole atmosphere in the class had shifted; students who had been snickering got right with the Lord real quick and sat quietly, eyes down. That sense of powerlessness made me feel, in a word, worthless. I had no control, and that was not the proper pecking order—I was supposed to be in charge. My students were looking to me to fix it, or at least react, and I couldn't. As they filed out of class, their looks of pity brought me to tears. They felt bad for me, and it was humiliating. I had worked so hard to create a safe, mutually respectful culture in my classroom, and one stupid act erased it.

So, during my planning period, I decided to do something I rarely did: I went to see my assistant principal. Seldom did I defer behavioral issues to administration; I preferred handling problems with students on my own, mindful that it was part of what helped create my classroom's culture. Me showing up red-faced in Mr. Pickmen's office was rare, and therefore enough to get his attention. Once I explained what had happened, we talked about the possible consequences. Three days' out-of-school suspension was a given for the student's behavior, but how did I want to handle the rest? I had every right to file a police report, Mr. Pickmen told me. He didn't sway me one way or the other; he simply informed me of my options. I paced his tiny office, wearing holes through the carpet.

"I don't think I want to involve the police." I sat down.

Whaaaaaaaaaaaat?! I silently screamed at myself. *A student pretends to hump you while you're teaching, and you don't want to file charges? You were clearly targeted because you're a woman and young and new, and you don't want to teach the kid a lesson? What will your inaction tell the other females in the building?*

"That is your decision," Mr. Pickmen said evenly. He called the student to his office.

When the student saw me, he wouldn't even look at me. He knew why he was there and offered an apology right away.

"Are you sorry for your behavior or that you got caught?" Mr. Pickmen's previously calm demeanor disappeared; he turned into an investigator grilling a suspect, enunciating every syllable as though they were the last the student would ever hear. "This woman has shown you nothing but respect. She gives her time and her energy to this school every single day, and this is how you treat her? You were new to our district a few years ago. Do you remember how hard it was to be new? It's no different for an adult, new to a job."

Damn. No wonder his name was on a plaque and stuff.

The student apologized again.

"Why? *Why* are you sorry?" my assistant principal pressed. I was sweating and I wasn't even the one in trouble.

"I'm sorry for doing what I did. It was wrong."

"Tell me what you did," Mr. Pickmen kept at him. "What did you do?"

I wanted to squeeze my eyes shut and evaporate into thin air; instead, I stared at the wall. I didn't want to hear the kid say it. Turns out, he couldn't. Either the gravity of the situation or his conscience kicked in, and he couldn't say the words.

Mr. Pickmen lowered his voice. "Do you know why you can't say it? I do. Because it feels wrong saying those things in front of a teacher, doesn't it? If it feels wrong to say it, you know it's wrong to do it. Now," he said, turning to me, "do you want to press charges?"

The student looked like he was going to vomit. I straightened my shoulders and pretended I wasn't about to do the same. I forced eye contact with the kid: "I know it's my right to press charges; what you did is sexual harassment and it's absolutely unacceptable. Do you understand?"

"Yes, ma'am."

"Even though it's my right, I'm not going to."

The kid exhaled.

Mr. Pickmen continued, "Even though it's her right, she's not going to involve the police. Do you understand there are other teachers in this building who would gladly have you kicked out for doing what you did?"

"Yes, sir."

"I'd say you're pretty lucky."

"Yes, sir."

"After your three-day suspension, I will be escorting you back to that class and you will apologize to *everyone*. You disrespected and embarrassed all those students, not just their teacher. Now get your things from your locker and get out."

I wanted to kiss Mr. Pickmen's shiny bald head in that moment. I'd been afraid to ask for his help, and assumed deferring to him would compromise the authority I had tried so hard to establish, but as I walked back to my classroom that day, I felt strangely empowered. Mr. Pickmen had given me choices and supported whatever I chose. He put the ball in my court and let me be a part of the solution. I wasn't deferring; I was deciding, and that is the epitome of authority.

While it was frustrating to engage in the same conversations over and over with the nurse, parents and students because of my age, I began to recognize the value in them. Each conversation helped build a new relationship, and it was through those relationships that I was able to solidify a reputation for being hard but fair, a reputation I certainly needed if I wanted any chance of effectively teaching people only a couple years younger than me. Finally, I stopped viewing my age as a detriment and understood how it had been helping me the whole time: Being such a young teacher gave me a unique perspective, one that allowed me to better empathize with students. After all, it wasn't that long ago I was the kid doing dumb things, praying some kind soul would grant me a second chance. Thank the maker social media wasn't all the rage when I was a teenager, that's all I'm sayin'.

Even though a bunch of my colleagues were aghast I hadn't pushed for stronger consequences to address such foul behavior, I stood by my decision. Passing the buck never works when dealing with kids, and that is what our students are: kids. Kids learn from their mistakes and since I'm in the business of teaching, it makes sense not to write them off for making one.

A Teacher's Sixth Sense: I See Dead Dogs

My sophomore English class was knee-deep in Homer's *The Odyssey*, an epic poem that can be an epic flop because it requires instruction with a certain *je ne sais quoi*. That's French for "ignore all the weird sex stuff."

The poem basically invites pandemonium, but by god, we are teachers! It's a requirement of the job to wrangle chaos and fight the battle against distractions. We roll with the punches when someone pulls the fire alarm during an exam. We persevere when a student throws up in the hallway right outside our classroom. We remain patient as our secretary confuses the new phone system with the PA system, interrupting the entire school with "announcements" of "Good afternoon, this is Hill High School" seventeen times a day. And so it was with thoughtful preparation and teamwork that my co-teacher and I were determined to keep the students focused on Odysseus and his journey.

We were busy redirecting student questions, such as "Is

Odysseus really boning a goddess?" and "Are Trojan condoms named after this story?" when I saw it.

Outside, at the base of a tree . . .

What the . . .

Multitasking as teachers do, I continued the class discussion while stealthily moving across the room, closer to the row of windows.

"Okay, someone talk to me about Greek hospitality." I sneaked a better look.

Half-listening to a student's response, I zeroed in on a lump half-buried beneath the thawing snow.

"Excellent! Now tell me about potential consequences for violating a host's hospitality." I ran through a mental checklist of all the things that could be at the base of that tree. Finally, I succumbed to the cold, hard reality: It was a dead dog.

To say that I *might* be a dog lover is like saying Justin Bieber *might* be the next *E! True Hollywood Story*: no doubt about it. When I cast my eyes on the poor pup's limp body a mere 30 feet away, my heart dropped and an internal panic gripped me.

Zillions of thoughts swarmed around in my head.

OMG, was that someone's pet?

Did the poor thing freeze to death?

We can't let the students see this!

DO. NOT. CRY.

The snow was melting under the afternoon sun; soon the morbid scene would be uncovered for everyone to see. And if there was one more distraction during this freaking poem,

Odysseus would really never get home.

Discreetly, I caught my coteacher's attention using only "teacher eyes."

Comparable to "parent eyes" in that they quietly suggest corrective action, "teacher eyes" are used to communicate a potential problem without interrupting the flow of instruction. In this case, my heads-up message was, "A canine kicked the bucket right over there, and I am panicking. Make note of this atrocity, but don't let it register on your face. Also, *What are we gonna do now?!*"

Her subtle nod let me know she understood.

My partner-in-classroom-crime skillfully held the students' attention by comparing the Sirens in the poem to the Kardashians, allowing me to inconspicuously slip to the back of the room and call our principal.

In hindsight, a call to the head honcho was maybe not so necessary. Coulda called the maintenance department, maybe even the secretary, but let's be honest: She would've answered the call over the loudspeaker and announced the situation to the entire building. Being the calm professional that I am, I made this call instead:

Me, breathy and creepy: "Umm, hi. There is a dead dog—I repeat, a dead dog—right outside of my window. I can't let the kids see, and I'm kinda freaking out!"

Head Principal: "Stay calm. Where exactly is the dog?"

Me: "In the woods, just beyond my farthest window."

Best Principal EVER: "I'm on it."

I hung up the phone and made "it's-being-handled" eyes

at my faithful collaborator. Never breaking our instructional stride, we continued teaching, and the students were none the wiser.

Until.

Our maintenance man, whom I loved dearly but was admittedly not the subtlest, clomped past our window in his knee-high rubber boots carrying a giant black garbage bag and what appeared to be a spear he had whittled out of a yardstick. Of course, the students noticed and all hard work at holding their attention was obliterated.

"He 'bout to shank somebody with that thing!"

"No, no! Everything's fine! Nothing to see out there—let's chat about how Odysseus cheats on his wife with some witch!"

No dice. The students watched, oblivious that our maintenance man was approaching a pile o' death. To my horror, he prodded the lifeless heap of fur with his pointy stick. Circling it, he poked from all different angles. Squatting down, his eyes narrowed, examining the scene like a CSI investigator. His hand hovering just above the mound, he lifted his head, searching for me. Once we made eye contact, a foreboding smile slowly crept across his face, and then he did the unthinkable. My hand instinctively flew to my mouth, muffling the gasp that escaped as he retrieved the dead dog and held it up like a trophy for everyone to see. Never breaking our gaze, he stood, victorious, clutching the garbage bag, prodding stick and a soggy, matted pile of dead . . . leaves.

Soooo . . .

Turns out the dog wasn't so much a dog as a messy mound of foliage left over from the fall. Minor detail.

I turned from the window, this time refusing to make eye contact with my coteacher, who wanted nothing more than to laugh in my face. Instead, I took advantage of the blessed fact that the students were clueless about what had just unfolded and refocused everyone's attention back to the lesson.

"Alrighty, back to work!"

A few minutes later, my classroom phone rang. Another interruption of the lesson and of my blatant attempt at denial.

Principal: "How's that dead dog situation?"

Me: "I'm sorry, I can't talk right now. I'm teaching the youth of America on the taxpayers' dime."

Principal: "You know I'm telling everyone about this, right?"

Me: "Yup."

I sure did cause a lot of confusion that day, unnecessarily alarming my coteacher and head principal and unwittingly sending our maintenance man on a wild goose (dog?) chase. My mistake, of course, disrupted the very lesson on which we'd gone to great lengths to keep the students' attention. I also embarrassed myself at school . . . again. Whatever. The moral of this story is the students, much like Odysseus, finally completed their odyssey despite the many challenges and crazy distractions that tried to throw them off course.

Yes, let's go with that. It's much more academic than my dumb ass confusing leaves for a dead dog.

Teacher Tip

If you're the favorite among students, make sure it's because you challenge and inspire them, not because you're too easy and lenient. Students will learn to interpret the latter as "my teacher didn't expect much of me."

Perspiration, Education, Transformation

Twenty-three: the number of interviews I went on in the first month after earning my teaching degree.

Zero: the number of jobs I was offered.

My confidence was waning when the universe finally threw me a bone; I applied to teach a five-week summer school program and was hired on the spot. After all my failed interviews, I was pleasantly surprised at the ease with which I landed the summer school gig. Years later, I would learn to recognize that kind of immediacy as a red flag. A warning that, perhaps, no one else was dumb/crazy/desperate enough to accept it. But at that point in my nonexistent career, I was just happy to earn me a paycheck. I was willing to look past the things that would've likely sent more seasoned educators running. Like the things I encountered on the first day of class:

- The vocational building where summer school would take place didn't have many traditional classrooms. There was a salon, welding shop and carpentry room, but instructional space was hard to come by. Therefore, my "classroom" was a 20-by-20-foot conference room with no air-conditioning.
- By nine a.m., June temperatures can climb into the 80s in a 20-x-20 non-air-conditioned room.
- My students were "at-risk" sophomores and juniors from a place called Hill High School. The other teachers informed me that "at-risk" was code for "behavior issues."
- Instructional materials were sparse, evidenced by the decrepit chalkboard on wheels, single stack of composition paper and two lonely boxes of pencils that greeted me that day.
- I would have to buy my own chalk.

Okay, so it wasn't the brightly lit classroom with overflowing resources of my dreams, but I could make do! I printed my name neatly on the chalkboard, making sure to hold it steady with one hand so it didn't flip over or roll away. Soon thereafter, my first-ever group of students walked through the door.

To break the ice, or more accurately, the melted pool of pee-warm water thanks to zero airflow in the room, we gave elevator speeches. Everyone had two minutes to introduce themselves; students had to tell me their names, why they ended up in summer school and anything else they wanted to share.

I listened as one student after another revealed the common denominator among them: They were in summer school because they quite simply didn't feel like going to school during the regular year. As one said, "Why do one hundred and eighty days when you can bang it out in five weeks?!"

Huh.

It was honestly the first time I had considered what is all too apparent now: Not all students go to school when they're supposed to or even care about getting good grades.

#PrivilegeCheck

So many of them came from broken homes, worked random jobs to help support their families, had already witnessed excessive violence or had parents who were addicts or incarcerated. It seemed as though the "at-risk" label didn't fairly represent them. They weren't bad kids who couldn't learn. The more I got to know them, the more I understood why school was not their priority.

It also became glaringly obvious that my college courses had not prepared me for this: I'd never worked with anything less than obedient students with few extenuating circumstances, not to mention the built-in support system of professors, facilitators and master teachers. I'd gone to college for four years, yet it took less than 60 minutes with these summer school students to teach *me* how to teach *them*.

I quickly revised my lesson plans for the week:

~~Parts of Speech Fun: Adjectives vs. Adverbs~~	*Get them excited about learning.*
~~Figurative Language: Similes & Metaphors, Oh My!~~	*Show them they are capable.*
~~SAT Vocabulary Words~~	*Prove I care.*

School was officially in session.

They didn't buy in immediately. If I wanted them to learn *my* content, I'd have to present it *their* way. I tailored assignments and lessons around their interests and lives. We dissected current music for figurative language and word choice, analyzed the local newspaper for any sign of bias in writing and wrote personal essays.

Those essays were our culminating project and they were exhausting. I pushed and prodded and begged those kids to put their hearts on paper, and at the end of each day, I felt as if I'd run a mental marathon. The students had always been responsible for learning, not teaching, and there I was asking them to teach me about their story. That kind of vulnerability made some of them uncomfortable and they lashed out, initially refusing to do the assignment. I understood the anger was their fear talking, fear that their story wasn't worthwhile because it was messy and hard. I gave them space, then tiptoed back to gently encourage, and we did this dance for a while. By the end of the summer school session, all but one student had written an essay and I considered that a win.

We had finally arrived at a place of mutual respect and trust. They understood I was trying my best, and so they tried their best, entrusting me with their stories. I was thrilled when they agreed to read their essays aloud. A student who struggled with stuttering asked if he could rap his essay, explaining reading made him nervous, but rapping felt natural. I sat back and listened as a room full of sixteen- and seventeen-year-olds read (and rapped) about their personal triumphs and losses, fears and dreams. I choked up again and again as they discovered their voices, owning their stories with a renewed sense of pride.

As promised, I shared an essay, too. I'd written about my recent interview-binge, divulging the embarrassing secret that I'd been passed over by more than 20 different school districts. When one of my favorite students (teacher, please, you know you have your favorites, too) announced his school, Hill High School, was currently hiring an English teacher, I gestured dramatically to my essay and laughed. I joked, "Maybe you missed the part about how I'm physically incapable of getting hired!" and expected nods of solidarity, but they were unfazed.

"So? Try again."

Their hard knocks were unimpressed with my pity party. You fall down, you get back up. Period.

"Fine," I agreed, "I'll make you a deal: If you write résumés and participate in mock job interviews as a final exam, I'll apply to your school."

They were in.

It wasn't a conscious decision, but I approached the Hill High School interview differently than I had all my others. Before Hill High, I had been concerned about looking and sounding the part, dressed in a power suit and purposefully including proper educational buzzwords in my responses. This time, though, I had actual experience on my side and mentioned students by name, finally able to recognize the need and joy of personalizing education. I'd also come to the interview directly after teaching in the hotbox that was my summer classroom, so no power suit. Instead, I rocked flip-flops and a professional-ish top that allowed my armpits to breathe. I inadvertently slipped in some of the students' slang when answering questions and was relieved when the principals laughed!

I didn't take the teaching portfolio I'd made as a college graduation requirement either; this time, I brought the students' essays. I confessed how difficult it had been to extract personal narratives from the kids but celebrated the ultimate success of our endeavor. When I shared the story of the boy who rapped his essay, I immediately felt my throat tighten with emotion again. I felt many things during that interview, but never once nervous. Everything felt natural, like it all belonged. Like I belonged.

Later that week, I sat in the sun on my parents' deck and expected exactly nothing.

And that's when the phone rang.

It was the head principal who had giggled when I referenced Kanye West in response to one of her questions.

Me: "I'm sorry, I didn't quite catch that last thing you said."

Principal: "I said, 'We want you. You got the job!'"

Me: "Duuuuuuuuuhhhhhh . . ."

Principal: "I get it. It's an exciting time, and I'm going to give you a lot of information that you'll need to digest, so just listen and then contact me when you realize you have questions."

She said so many words, but the ones that have stuck with me to this day were: "Hill High School students need someone like you."

The following day was the last of our summer school session. I arrived early to write one final note on the rickety chalkboard: a game of Hangman. Surprised to see how many students decided to attend the day notorious for excessive absences, dressed in their mock interview best, I beamed as they filed into our room, looking quizzically at the dashes on the chalkboard.

"Okay, go! Throw some letters at me!"

They began shouting out *A*'s and *R*'s and *L*'s, and finally completed the puzzle before the chalk man met his demise: "I am a Hill High Warrior, too!"

Those students applauded. *They cheered for me.* Kids who didn't give a damn about school a month ago were now visibly excited about something school-related. And oh, did it feel good! I considered what the principal had said: Hill High School students needed a teacher like me. While that may have been true, she couldn't possibly have known I needed those students just as much. Before them, I was a walking, talking textbook, confident that the content knowledge would beget my professional success. What I hadn't taken into account was the part of teaching that makes it so personal, the part that makes every single day worth it—the students. My first Hill High School students shaped who I became as an educator, teaching me more about the profession than any college course ever could. And that's the beauty of teaching: Amid the whirlwind of yet another initiative, funding woes or unsupportive administration, the students will always bring us back to center, reminding us why we chose the profession in the first place.

If my summer school experience taught me anything, it's that sometimes, we have to suffer through a little perspiration to arrive at our inspiration.

Education Is More Than a Single Story

H i, I'm a white lady, and I'd like to talk to you about race. If you're reading this, there's a good chance you're also a white person. I've surmised this based on the fact that about 80 percent of United States teachers are, in fact, white, and because this book is largely written for educators, I've deduced my audience is overwhelmingly Caucasian. My husband, an AP statistics teacher (also white!), tells me that's not how statistics work. I told him he can just go ahead and write his own book.

It's not always easy talking about issues involving race, but I think the conversation is too important to ignore just because it's hard. We're going to have to get uncomfortable and squirm in our seats a little if we're serious about improving our schools. I'm going to use words like *privilege* and *racism* and "Clair Huxtable" and I need you to promise you'll pay attention. My eight-year-old daughter says we have to pinkie-promise or I can't believe you. Go ahead and press your pinkie to this page. I'll wait.

My parents never openly chatted about such things as institutional racism or social inequality. We were privileged that life didn't force us to have those conversations. I didn't even realize issues like that existed because Clair Huxtable never told me about them on *The Cosby Show*. Weren't all nonwhite families wealthy with two successful parents and a mom who could dole out discipline with nothing more than The Look? Gah, I loved me some Clair! As I got older, I was shocked to learn the truth via different sources: news stories, hip-hop lyrics and an outspoken high school class-mate. As one of thirteen nonwhite kids in our class of 350, my pal April advised I *really* pay attention to what we were learning: Our curriculum was "whitewashed," history books were not exactly thorough when discussing black and brown contributions, and aside from *To Kill a Mockingbird*, litera-ture didn't afford many opportunities to explore cultural and social issues. Unless you counted Victorian England, which I did not.

My point is this: I came from a place of ignorance in the very truest sense of the word. Not until I chose to pay attention did I realize my reality wasn't the same as everyone else's, the very definition of white privilege. It was like living next door to the same neighbors for years and then one day realizing I'd never stepped foot inside their home. It wasn't until April invited me in that I began understanding how institutional racism is responsible for countless disparities in nonwhite communities, including educational opportunities.

This is why I task educators to open doors and invite the hard conversations inside.

Once I was hired at Hill High School, April's request to pay attention to what we were learning echoed in my ears. This time, in my role as the teacher, I was also paying attention to *how* we were learning. It didn't take long to recognize that my students' backgrounds significantly impacted the way they reacted to and processed their education. We were a Title I school, meaning we served a large population of families who struggled with poverty, many of whom were African American. Despite the clear-cut demographics of the students, our school didn't do a very good job of representing them. The curriculum was rather exclusive, factoring in people of color only as slaves or Native Americans. Novel choices in our English classes remained dominated by white protagonists and narratives, likely the culprit of students' disconnect from their assigned readings.

I was fortunate enough to work with a fabulously progressive and open-minded department chair at Hill High. She had already begun laying the groundwork for change, and together, our English teachers rewrote our department's entire curriculum. We selected more inclusive stories, such as Walter Dean Myers's *Monster* and "The Danger of a Single Story" by Chimamanda Ngozi Adichie. We incorporated more research-based projects that encouraged students to learn about different cultures, using TED Talks to introduce people and ideas that may have otherwise been overlooked.

It's certainly not my intention to insinuate nonwhite is synonymous with being economically disadvantaged. It's just that my experiences are with a very specific group of students, and so, too, is this essay. I acknowledge the limitations inherent within those experiences.

Personal limitations notwithstanding, what I've learned about race and education over the last two decades is too important not to share. Some of these lessons include actionable items, others require dreaded introspection on our part, but promise me you'll do it even if it makes you uncomfortable. Gimme that pinkie finger. . . .

"At-risk" is a dangerous term.

Students who are considered at-risk are characterized as such by factors they can't control: skin color, how much money their family makes, where they live. Trust me, students are well aware when they're poor and live in the bad section of town. Why slap on another socially disadvantageous label to make sure they also know schools expect them to fail? While I appreciate the intention to identify kids who need extra support because they absolutely need more thoughtful, intentional instruction, this terminology is below the belt. Be cognizant of how a label can impact a kid's design to learn.

Note: "At-risk" is still so engrained in educational vernacular that I had to use it in this book for the sake of clarification. Brainstorming session starts now: Let's call kids . . . by their names. Done.

Care. For real.

I don't have to tell you students know when we're faking. They can sniff out disingenuous dudes like a bloodhound picking up a scent. They know the difference between a teacher who's in the classroom every day and a teacher who shows up for them every day. Honest relationships are essential, and we've got to take the time to build them. If that doesn't sound like something you want to do, ask yourself why. Is it because you've had bad experiences with different cultures and races? Be honest and ask yourself another question: Is it possible you're harboring prejudice and bias that are impacting your relationships with students? There's no law forcing us to like everyone, but if you continually bump heads with those who don't look like you, I'm thinking it's time for some of that introspection.

Hoodies aren't bad, so stop it.

"Why don't you take the tags off your clothes?" I once asked a student, figuring he was showing off his shoplifting skills. He then schooled me in hip-hop fashion and I felt old and very guilty for assuming the worst of him. But I learned something and that's the point. We may not appreciate or understand our students' fashion choices (what is with all the holes in the upper thighs of jeans today?!), but for the love of all that is caffeinated, we cannot assume to know anything about their character based on their attire.

Expand the narrative.

If you can't change the curriculum by choosing new texts or novels, at least expand the narrative to include contributions from other cultures and races. We can do better than just slavery and the civil rights movement! Let's celebrate our multicultural heroes, inventors and scholars. Moreover, it's important we don't shy away from class discussions that include current social issues. Not allowing students to voice their opinions or concerns is essentially telling them their feelings don't matter. Create a safe space for your learners to share and lead discussions with a sensitive authority so everyone can reap the built-in benefits of learning about different perspectives.

Challenge them.

Do not see "at-risk" or skin color and assume it has anything to do with students' *ability* to learn. Too many schools automatically lower their academic or behavioral standards, when they need to do the opposite and set the bar higher for these kids. Give them the proper tools and support and watch them rise to the occasion.

We need more nonwhite teachers.

A majority of U.S. teachers are white, while almost 50 percent of our students are nonwhite. That gap will continue to grow unless we get more nonwhite teachers in our schools. I'm not insinuating just any educator of color. Please refer to the "Care. For real." section to review the importance of building sincere relationships with students. And don't get all offended, white teachers; you and I do a great job of loving our students and advocating for their learning. It's just that statistics prove African American kids in particular reap many educational benefits from having quality African American teachers. Actually, having just *one* inspirational Black teacher as early as elementary school can mean the difference between a Black student graduating from high school or not.

We also need cultural consciousness trainings.

In the words of rapper DMX, "y'all gon' make me lose my mind up in here." I'm talking to you, school districts that haven't updated their professional development series since 2001. Let's get real and talk about cultural competence and diversity. Let's hold teachers accountable for learning about their students' backgrounds. Let's leave the confines of our schools and venture into the surrounding communities where our students are spending most of their time. Let's just talk about something other than using rubrics. *Please.*

Forge bonds with students' families.

Figure out who your student's "person" is and make him or her your ally. Could be a parent, grandma, someone from church or a neighbor. Whoever it is, invite that person to be an active participant in the kid's education.

Acknowledge your own privilege.

If you hear the phrase *white privilege* and immediately feel insulted, the best thing to do is get over yourself. Privilege comes in many forms: money, education, knowledge, gender and skin color, to name a few. The sooner we understand how *not* having enough of or the right kinds of those things impedes a student's access to educational opportunities, the more successful we'll be in the classroom.

Provide opportunities they wouldn't otherwise have.
So many of our students don't realize the opportunities that await within their respective communities. I cannot express how very important it is to provide as many artistic and cultural experiences as possible while these kids are in our schools. If traveling isn't feasible, consider bringing groups and organizations to your schools. Museums, libraries, city cultural districts and art centers are exceptionally accommodating. Help build students' background knowledge; just one taste of possibility can light that fire for a kid. Make it happen.

Be aware and empathetic.
People of color continue to struggle with injustice and inequality in ways many of us will never personally experience. As such, it's essential we're aware of what's going on in our students' lives, because it absolutely affects how they learn. While this is certainly true for all our students, it's simply not accurate to say all students will be affected firsthand by things like immigration or the impetus for the Black Lives Matter movement. Awareness and empathy are equally as important as our instructional methods and assessment tools. It is our

job to support and educate every single student, and to do so effectively, we must address their emotional needs as well as their academic ones.

Read between the lines.

When I was in junior high school, I got caught shoplifting. As the store manager berated me for disrespecting his business, I laughed. *Laughed!* Infuriated, he started yelling and swearing. I then asked him to please lower his voice and watch his language. <insert shocked face emoji here.> Despite my cool, arrogant exterior, internally I was—excuse the expression— shitting bricks. It's really hard for some of us to be vulnerable, so we do this weird thing where we cover up fear with an angry blanket. Couple that with hormonal adolescence, and you've got yourself the perfect storm. Much to my husband's chagrin, I still manage to default to "the blanket" even today. I never considered it a viable personality trait until it helped me understand some of my students. I'm able to interpret their infuriating laughter for what it really is: an attempt to conceal weakness or embarrassment. When they say, "I don't care!" I hear, "I'm afraid I'm not smart enough." Breaking through those tough exteriors isn't easy, but it's worth it. Just ask my husband.

We all know the key ingredient to successfully interacting with all kinds of people is basic human decency. Some of us unfortunately have a hard time maintaining that decency when working with cultures different from ours, and therein lies the problem. We signed up to be teachers because we care about kids! I know most of us do what we need to in order to reach our students and be mindful of their backgrounds, so I applaud us and encourage us to keep doing good work. I won't lie, though, some of you are shady! Why choose a profession in education if you're not willing to set aside your ego for the sake of every child's learning? If among those, may I suggest looking for employment elsewhere? You're bringing the rest of us down.

This concludes a white lady's talk on race and education.

That's Just My Gallbladder Exploding

On a good day, I can pee after third period. I teach for three consecutive hours, which is hard to do after morning coffee, but I've trained my bladder to expect release around 11:15 a.m. Afternoon bathroom breaks are more difficult, as many factors tend to interfere: I usually spend my lunch in my room, proofing yearbook photos or having students make up tests, then I'm on lunch duty (pray for me), then I teach for another three consecutive hours. Most days I can't get to a restroom until my plan period, which is at the very end of the day, but if I have to cover another teacher's class, my bladder is on the verge of bursting by 2:50 p.m. each afternoon.

Because I'm an intelligent woman who doesn't want to pee herself in public, I have learned the exact amount of water I can consume during this length of time to keep me properly hydrated and avoid unplanned potty breaks: 12 ounces. It was trial and error at first; too much water had me running to the restroom during or in between classes, leaving a room full of teenagers to their own devices. *No bueno.* Too little water and my throat turned into the Sahara Desert, burning and aching with every word I croaked. I must abide by the 12 ounces or the delicate balance of my bladder is severely compromised.

I imagine teachers are among the few professionals forced to schedule their bodily functions this way. If a banker needs to tinkle, he puts up a "be right back" sign. If a doctor's breakfast burrito kicks in, his patients simply wait. Most other working folks have the luxury of being able to indulge a leisurely BM whenever the mood strikes, but teachers? Not so much.

That's why when the sudden onslaught of pain hits, the last thing I think to do is head to the bathroom. *This is not an appointed restroom time! Must power through!* But the next jolt of pain takes my breath away and I begin considering running for the nearest toilet. Only problem is, now I can barely stand. One hand clutches the tests I had been returning while the other white-knuckles the side of a student's desk. I steel myself against the imaginary switchblade that continuously stabs at me with swift sharpness. I am grateful that teenagers are notoriously self-absorbed; none of them seem to notice I am dying a slow, painful death right before their eyes.

Even if it were a previously scheduled break, heading to the bathroom isn't even an option at this point. I have to *sit* down before I *fall* down. I make my way over to the mile-high stack of papers, also known as my desk, and gingerly lower myself into the chair. Doubled over in agony, as though an angry kung fu kangaroo is repeatedly drop-kicking me in the gut, I keep thinking, "Don't scare the kids.

You're fine. Take deep breaths." Except I am not fine, and the deep breaths aren't helping. I'm about four seconds from full-on panic mode when, fortunately, the dismissal bell rings. Unfortunately, I'm now drenched in sweat and unable to bear my own weight, certain of my imminent demise. Even more unfortunate is that my homeroom students have begun filing in, and this time there's no chance they aren't going to notice what's going on. One look at me and they stop in their tracks.

Eyes wide, fearful, no one says a word until one brave soul ventures, "You don't look so good, Mrs. J." I force a smile while politely explaining my predicament, leaving out the part about my imminent demise.

"Can we help you? Should we call the nurse?"

Please recall our school nurse. The one who mistook me for a hall-wandering student on more than one occasion and got all up in my face about it. In short, the nurse and I weren't exactly pals.

Back to the story.

Observing the worry in my students' faces but knowing I can't manage the few feet to the phone, I do the only rational thing and ask someone to push my desk chair—with me in it—across the room so I can make the call.

As we're waiting for Nurse Ratched's arrival, the students and I engage in awkward conversation to ignore the fact I've turned ashen and sweat has saturated my hair, matting it against my face and neck. As the chills set in, we chat about what the cafeteria is serving for lunch.

"The pizza is like rubber!"

"Why's stuff gotta be so expensive when it sucks?!"

"We need a KFC or McDonald's up in here."

Finally, and with urgency normally reserved for delivering babies that have already partially delivered themselves, the school nurse bursts into our classroom, pushing a wheelchair. Demonstrating her competency in emergency situations, she immediately begins shrieking at the kids: *"Back up! Give her space!"* And then at me: *"Are you breathing okay? Can you walk?!"* My students fall over themselves trying to clear her a path, fully convinced they are about to witness my untimely departure from this earth. An act of God helps transfer me from the desk chair to the wheelchair.

And we're off.

I have never seen our school nurse move at a pace one would consider brisk. Kids have been bleeding, kids have passed out, but this woman has one speed and it ain't quick. Some say she's a bit lazy; others maintain she's mentally checked out and ready for retirement. There is lore, though, that some have witnessed an accelerated gait upon departing from her office to enjoy all three lunch periods. I can't speak to the latter, but I will say that day, when I needed her most, she moved like the fucking wind. Her freshly polished white orthopedic shoes slapping the cement floors is a sound I shall carry with me always.

Once we're in her office, she looks bewildered.

What to do now?

She touches my forehead and immediately wipes her now sweat-soaked hand on her pant leg. She takes my temperature, then asks the same set of questions three times. Finally,

I suggest we call my emergency contact, as I'd like to get my sweaty ass to the hospital. Because my husband is at work, I opt to call my mother, temporarily forgetting how terrible she is in crisis situations. She tends not to focus on said crisis, but on extraneous yet controllable details. As I'm wondering why I've even listed her as an emergency contact, she answers the phone:

Me: Don't freak out, but I'm pretty sick and need you to pick me up. We have to go to the emergency room.

Mom: I haven't even gotten a shower yet!

Me: That's okay, no one in the ER will care.

Mom: Do I have time to throw on makeup?

Me: You do not.

Mom: Can I—

Me: MOM.

She hangs up, knowing I'm not the type to cry wolf. In the sixth grade, I experienced my first ocular migraine. When I suddenly couldn't see the multiplication problem on the chalkboard, I yelled out, "I'm blind! Somebody help me!"

Guess who else doesn't do well in crisis situations?

Despite living approximately five miles from our elementary school, it had taken my mom a good 30 minutes to show up that day. It had been her day off, and she was none too pleased I had interrupted it. The second we walked out of the school and into the blazing sunshine, I threw up all over the blacktop where my classmates would soon be jumping rope and playing kickball. "Told ya," I said, wiping my mouth. She apologized profusely and never doubted me again.

I envision her now, like a bungling NASCAR driver, speeding to my rescue.

While I wait, I figure I should let my husband know what's going on, but rather than worry him, I simply ask his secretary to give him a message:

"Hi, this is Zach's wife and I'm headed to the emergency room. I'm not sure what's wrong, there's a lot of pain, but he doesn't need to meet me or anything, just make sure he goes home right after work to let the dogs out."

Priorities.

Twenty minutes later, my frantic mother—who has applied mascara—comes sprinting into the building. The nurse explains I must be wheeled to the waiting car. This means I am a one-woman parade for all the students currently heading to the cafeteria to behold.

I'm embarrassed because I've sweated through my clothes, but I'm also scared because, *dying*. Not really knowing what to do or how to act, I kind of wave to everyone. "Hi there, everything is fine," I lie. One student calls after me as I head out the main doors: "It'll be okay, Mrs. J! I'll pray for you!" I would love to tell you that made me feel so much better, but in that moment, I was sure I had just crapped my pants. So much for those scheduled bathroom breaks, eh?

The fresh air feels good on my greasy face and provides a bit of relief. Then I remember my mom doesn't think or drive well under pressure . . . and she's my ride to the hospital. I begin praying my student really is praying and has invited everyone else to pray along with him.

In approximately 70 seconds, we arrive at the hospital ten miles away.

I'm seen immediately, tests are run and it is determined my gallbladder is "diseased." Although it hasn't burst (*yay!*), it would have to be removed (*boo!*), especially if the husband and I had any plans of getting pregnant in the near future. Since we'd recently added *have unprotected sex* to our summer to-do list, I make the appointment for surgery. Contrary to my opinion, the doctor deems the situation nonemergent and sends me home with a note and enough pain medication to sedate an African bush elephant.

Miraculously, I wake the next morning feeling almost back to normal. Since my sick days are limited, I decide to save them for postsurgery recovery and head into work. Plus, I now have an ace up my sweaty sleeve and the freedom to play it when necessary.

Everyone is surprised to see me upright so soon after my near-death experience. Most are relieved I'm well; others seem disappointed I didn't kick the bucket. Before making my way to my classroom, I pay my principal a visit and present my doctor's note. With wide eyes and an excited smile, I hand over the note. "Get a load of this!" I gush.

My principal reads it and looks at me with an amused smirk. "Explicit permission to use the bathroom on demand, huh? And I thought you were just excited to be alive."

Teacher Tip

You can't fix stupid (I'm talking about other adults), so don't stress over the things you can't control. And again, I'm talking about the adults.

Throw a Chair at Your Colleague! And Other Conflict-Resolution Don'ts

This one time, my colleague came to work drunk.

Which means, a teacher came to school drunk.

Therefore, students witnessed a drunk teacher at school.

I won't lie: Part of me was all, "I wanna be drunk, too!" Teaching is a stressful job that has me at my wit's end on the regular, but laws and personal pride help me make better decisions than imbibing before arriving.

Anyway, the teacher was subsequently sent home and the rest of us were instructed on how to properly field the incessant questions from students. I reminded myself we all make mistakes; hello, dead dog! Also, I had no idea what was happening in the teacher's personal life that would compromise her common sense to such an extent. I tried putting myself in her boozy shoes, feeling sorry for her because the impending consequences for such egregious behavior would undoubtedly be significant.

Except the teacher returned the next day as though nothing had happened. There were no repercussions for her and not one apology from her. Not even an acknowledgment that the rest of us had been team players who covered her class and her ass. Everyone knows teachers live in a fishbowl and that we're held to higher standards than our profess-ional counterparts. Fair or not, that's just the way it is for us. Without so much as an "I'm sorry," this colleague selfishly put us all in a position of having to defend our reputations with nary an ounce of accountability. And that enraged me.

Not that I could do anything about it. I had no authority over a fellow teacher, and who was I to question the outcome? So I did what I always do: complained to my husband at home. As is our custom, we'd end up laughing at all the inappropriate things I fantasized about doing or saying at work.

During the school day, when the stresses of teaching got to be too much, I reverted back to quietly concocting new and unprofessional ways I'd love to conduct myself. Throat punch a parent? Don't mind if I do! The following scenarios are a few of the conflict-resolution tips I created during a particularly rough year. You know those years: where the days each have 76 hours and you hate your job with every fiber of your being. Kindly note that these are examples of what I'd like to do if laws didn't apply and if I could turn thoughts into actions with impunity. Basically, these are terrible ideas and you shouldn't try them if you hope to maintain a shred of dignity or employment. Read them, laugh, share them with teacher friends and then go back to being the respectable educator we know you are.

Conflict: Coteaching sucks. Your coteacher is lazy and acts like another student instead of a fellow educator. You're tired of carrying the weight.
Resolution: Throw that coteacher right under the proverbial bus by not showing up to work for a whole week. Baptism by fire should do the trick.

Conflict: During a tense faculty meeting, the colleague who thrives on confrontation comes at you with her signature eye roll and condescending tone.
Resolution: Lunge at her from across three rows of chairs, but not before you've removed your earrings.

Conflict: Your assistant principal calls you into his office to discuss why Sally is failing your class, asking what *you* can do better. He conveniently leaves out the part about Sally missing 40 of the last 60 days of school.
Resolution: Suggest he drive Sally to school each day, personally escort her to your class and then sit beside her with a Taser in an effort to keep her on task. Or just laugh and laugh then walk out.

Schooled

Conflict: The football coach sends an email to all of the starting quarterback's teachers, requesting his grade be "bumped up by just a few percentage points" so he's eligible for next Friday's big game.
Resolution: Reply-all with a picture of your whole bare ass.

Conflict: The administration has implemented yet another program that results in funding for the school and a lot of additional work for the teachers, but no real academic benefits for the students.
Resolution: Stage a coup. Make signs. Call the local news. Light things on fire.

Conflict: A parent requests a meeting with you to "discuss" the failing grade you "gave" her student.
Resolution: In the 20 seconds you're allotted to speak, quickly define *plagiarism*. For the remainder of the 30 minutes the parent talks at you, appear uninterested as accusations fly that you have a personal vendetta against her special snowflake. I highly recommend playing Words with Friends or scrolling through Instagram during this time. At the meeting's conclusion, shrug apathetically and give the kid whatever grade the parent wants. It'll take less time and energy to wash your hands of the situation than to try to explain academic integrity to these morons.

Conflict: Class sizes increase as furloughs in your building continue. You now have more students than desks.
Resolution: Have IKEA furniture delivered care-of your superintendent of schools. Gather round as he attempts to assemble it.

Conflict: It's midyear and materials are already dwindling.
Resolution: Dressed as your school mascot, rob the local office supply store by brandishing the last extra-sharpened #2 pencil in a threatening fashion at the clerk. If you're going down, do it with flare.

Conflict: A student repeatedly disrespects you during class, refuses to do work and uses inappropriate language.
Resolution: Kick over desks while pounding your chest. Scream, "Who's head bitch in charge now?" until someone cries.

Conflict: Regardless of previous attempts to guard your time, the same colleague keeps interrupting your planning period.
Resolution: Keep a stash of water balloons in your desk drawer and fire away the second he opens your door. Optional: Fill balloons with ink, honey or other alternative substance of your choice.

Conflict: The guidance counselor pays you a visit three days before graduation, asking what you can do for Tim, a senior who hasn't turned in one assignment since February.
Resolution: Hand over all your instructional materials and congratulate the counselor on her new job as Tim's teacher.

An unwritten prerequisite of making it as a teacher is the ability to find the funny amid the frustrations. There is transformative power in laughter, even if our jokes grow more inappropriate in direct correlation with our stress levels. Teachers know a solid sense of humor can buoy us through even the most difficult times, which is probably why so many of us are closeted potty-mouths who appreciate semiviolent activities like ax throwing. What can I say? A teacher needs an outlet or she comes to work drunk.

Today's Kids

Traditionally, community members opt to run for school board positions because they want to be a part of the educational process. They become a voice for other families, representing every angle and perspective of important decisions. These men and women work long hours with no pay and are responsible for making critical choices that impact students, teachers and the entire community. Despite working a thankless and stressful job, school board members are ultimately committed to helping their schools run as smoothly as possible.

Unless they're power-hungry bullies with an ax to grind and a personal agenda to push.

Unfortunately, that was my first experience with school boards, back in 2003. I had been working in a high school where our head principal was a white woman and our assistant principal was a black man. Apparently, some members of the traditional small-town community struggled to accept our nontraditional administration, so much so that they decided to run for the school board. Under the guise of making our building a safer place, their entire fear-based campaign smeared our principals for being "too lax" when it came to enforcing such things as dress code and student conduct. But I knew the truth and so did many others; we saw right through the lies and concerned façade. Inspired by bigotry, these incoming board members simply wanted a woman and black man to remember their place, which was clearly not at the head of the table.

The deepening divide in the community began seeping into the school, oozing thick and heavy tension down the hallways. My colleagues and I tried shielding students from the underhanded political ploys, determined not to get involved. We agreed it had no place in the classroom, yet in our classrooms is exactly where it showed up.

I distinctly remember the night of parent-teacher conferences when one of the wannabe board members paid me a visit. I opened my classroom door to find what looked like the love child of Richard Simmons and Lenny from *Of Mice and Men*. Without a word, this big, burly fellow in an old-school tracksuit swished right past me and stuffed himself into one of the student desks. He was panting and dressed as if he had just finished a Zumba class, and were it not for the menacing look in his eyes, I would have appreciated the humor.

I shared my concern about the recent changes I'd seen in his daughter. Along with other campaigning board members' children, she had become withdrawn, sullen. Rather than address this topic, he asked whether I liked working for our principals. He made no secret about his disdain for our current administrators, and I made no secret about how the environment he was creating was bad for education. We should have been discussing open-ended essay prompts or even how his behavior was isolating and humiliating his child, but instead he promised change was coming. "A new broom sweeps clean" was his veiled threat.

He visited other teachers that night, unfortunately scoring a few allies along the way. That was all the fuel he needed to light the place on fire.

He and his posse were elected and by now, you can guess what their first order of business was. We had one month until the next meeting, where we knew the board would move to oust our principals. Our staff planned to be there, and apparently so did our students.

The night of the meeting, hundreds of people spilled into the conference room, forcing the board to move into the cafeteria to accommodate the unusually large crowd. The throng of students donning T-shirts and posters emblazoned with support for their principals moved me to tears. While we teachers had been caught up in our desire to protect instructional time and keep things "business as usual" for the sake of our students, they'd morphed into activists right under our noses. A group of seniors who were the living, breathing embodiment of our principals' educational investments over the last four years had begun organizing clandestine efforts of their own. They had designed the T-shirts, rallied classmates to attend the meeting and called the local newspaper to cover it all. We later learned these teenagers had also been meeting after school and on the weekends to craft and perfect the speeches they presented to the board that night.

When they took turns at the microphone, speaking sincerely and eloquently on behalf of the principals they loved, I cried openly and applauded them for having the courage to show up for their school.

Think about that for a second. We weren't at a football game. The meeting wasn't about prom. These young men and women gave freely of their time and voice for no other reason than to support a cause they were passionate about: education.

I listened in awe as one student after the other articulated emotions far too complicated for those twice their age to convey clearly. The English teacher in me proudly noted how carefully and purposefully students had selected their words, allowing them to communicate frustrations and opinions in a consistently respectful manner, a feat many of the board members were unable to accomplish that evening. Those kids were the doers of good that night, the righters of wrongs. They'd shown up, and after three hours, they knew they had been heard.

I'd love nothing more than to tell you our students changed the new board's mind that night. They didn't. Within days, a new position suddenly popped up and the urgency with which it had to be filled was nothing more than a red herring. It came as no surprise that our head principal was to be moved into that position and that it could be terminated at any moment, unlike a contracted administrative position. The writing was on the wall for our assistant principal. As the father of three young children, he had to worry about what his unemployment would mean for his family. He was soon hired at another district, and none of us could blame him.

One of the darkest moments in my teaching career collided with one of the brightest. For months after the meeting, that unforgiving juxtaposition compounded confusion and frustrations, not just for me, but throughout the entire school. We were heartbroken and angry that our efforts hadn't birthed the outcome we'd hoped for, but the experience revealed strengths and ignited passions we hadn't realized existed in students.

At a time when they should have been focused on graduation and final exams and playoff games—and when many would classify them as "lazy" or "checked out"—our students went to bat for the sake of their school. They were the epitome of strength and grace, and they are the reason I interrupt strangers when I overhear them bad-mouthing "today's kids" while at a restaurant or waiting in the doctor's office. Today's kids are nothing short of amazing and capable. I wish I knew more adults whose sense of purpose and clearly defined direction acted as their moral compass the way it does for "today's kids." As our school picked up the pieces and set out to rebuild, out of the rubble came a defining moment, at least for me: I will never doubt what today's kids can do.

Teacher Truth

You'll take much more than student work home with you at the end of the day.

No Degree Prepares You for a Permanent Good-Bye

The first year of teaching was, in a word, humbling. As a fresh college graduate, it became embarrassingly obvious that my education degree really only prepared me to deliver information. Like, I was ready to roll when it came to explaining subject-verb agreement, but no professor ever told me what to do when a student asks to use my phone to call for a ride home but actually schedules an appointment to have her nipples pierced.

Because teachers are taught to plan lessons by beginning with the end in mind, I took that advice very literally and forced myself to focus on getting students to the next step, whatever that next step was. I reasoned that since education is ultimately about progressing, it made sense to view each day as one step closer to an end goal. Sometimes the only goal was making it to Friday unscathed. More often, though, it was arriving at the finish line of a big project, a passing grade on an exam or even seeing students graduate and earn their own diplomas and bullshit sense of confidence, like I'd felt.

With this mentality, I was always looking ahead. Always planning. I became borderline obsessive in my laser focus, barreling toward our destination, the details along the way a blur.

I understand now that's part of the reason why her death jarred me the way it did. In all my incessant planning, my compulsive must-get-to-tomorrow approach to teaching, I'd never once considered tomorrow wasn't a guarantee.

She was only seventeen. First responders said she died instantly, and we found a strange solace in that fact, but regardless, it's excruciatingly unnatural for a young person's life to stop on a dime. Her passengers survived and eventually returned to school, though outwardly and inwardly scarred. The student's mom worked in our building and understandably did not return after the accident. Inside the walls of our school, time stopped. Reminders of our loss met us at every turn: grieving students, that unoccupied desk, one fewer smiling face in the hallway. An enormous feeling of emptiness consumed our school.

It now felt wrong to look ahead when one of our own no longer had that privilege. I fought with what I perceived as distinct contradictions of the job, caught between my own grief and the responsibility to teach. How could I be expected to continue teaching when our students were still mourning the loss of their classmate and friend? When a colleague had lost her child? How could students be expected to focus on school in the middle of a tragedy? My colleagues and I attempted to navigate unchartered territory, unsure of how or when to proceed. It seemed our entire building was being held captive by the stifling grip of uncertainty.

I grappled with this as I stood with my colleagues in the receiving line at the funeral home, the cacophony of a mother's wails drowning out all other thoughts. I must've phrased one too many of my concerns with "I just can't . . . " or "How can I . . . ?", because my principal whispered: "This isn't about you." Her words weren't malicious or biting. She recognized that emotions were clouding my judgment and, though unintentionally, I was overlooking the needs of others, namely those of my students, who needed the normalcy of their workday to return if only for the sake of processing their own grief.

The next day in class, I reminded students that grief counselors were available if needed, and we returned to the content. We would never forget our classmate, but we would have to find ways to honor her in our learning. Slowly, we would heal together.

I came to understand why those college courses only taught me about the what and how of education, and not the who: The who must be experienced firsthand, not learned. There's not a one-trick pony when it comes to teaching kids, no one-size-fits-all approach. Theoretically, I'd known that, but putting it all into practice seemed to require so much more than I was able, or maybe willing, to give. As a first-year teacher already suffering from imposter syndrome, I'd been telling myself to keep my head down and stay the course for now, assuming that I would eventually hit that sweet spot, where I'd be able to combine the content stuff and the kid stuff. I was buying time that didn't exist. I'd sacrificed experience for efficiency, and as a result, missed opportunities to truly connect with and enjoy the kids. I'm sad to say it took losing a student for me to realize this.

That student's funeral was the first, but unfortunately not the last, I would attend in my time as a teacher. Since that year, I've loosened the reins considerably, and instead of looking ahead so much, I try being present in the moment more often. Sure, we have benchmarks to meet and tests to take, but by focusing only on those things, I was missing out on some of the very best parts of teaching. I've slowed down and learned to appreciate what I used to consider unnecessary interruptions. When a student is off-topic during a class discussion, I let them forge their own temporary path, seizing the opportunity to build their character along with their vocabulary. I pump the brakes when students need a breather, inundated with testing stress. We talk about things like self-care and growth mindsets right along with schedules and graduation requirements.

Now, when I do look ahead, visions of a lesson's end goal are interspersed with daydreams of individual student successes. I've finally arrived at that sweet spot in my career, wherein relationships and learning are simultaneously nurtured. The emotional connections we create with our students are bonds that exist long after they leave our classroom. They are connections worth spending more time cultivating because they endure, even when we don't.

The Day Will Come When You'll Want to Quit, but You Shouldn't. Probably.

I wish I could do math in my head the way my husband (and ten-year-old son . . .) can.

I wish I could recall movie quotes or song lyrics for every occasion, a gift my brother, his steel-trap mind and impeccable comedic timing possess.

I wish I could pronounce the word "Worcestershire" without sounding like I have a mouth full of pennies. *Wish I could spell it without having to Google it, too.*

What's my point?

The point, fellow educator, is we all have wishes. Aspirations. Goals. And it can be a sad day in the classroom when the things we've worked so dang hard for don't come to fruition. When we give our all only to be told it's not enough; when we come in early and stay late and it seems to go unnoticed; when our creative, interactive lesson plans are replaced with teaching to the test; when we're made to redo the thing we just did because our superintendent is trying to impress other superintendents at some conference.

I get it.

The weight of frustration is heavy. If we're not careful, it can suffocate the passion that fueled us in the first place. That passion is why we're here, right? We want to make tomorrow better by working on today. We love kids and learning and teaching and inspiring and *ohmygoodness* those lightbulb moments are to die for!

I know, I know. It's way too easy to forget the passion—so many things are standing in the way:

- Lack of support from home and community
- Standardized testing pressure
- Student behavior issues
- Insufficient funding
- Implications of integrating ever-changing technology in the classroom
- Decreased academic success
- Difficulty engaging students
- High teacher and administrative turnover rates
- Transient students
- Not enough hours in the day
- Implementing new ways of doing things just to say we're doing new things

- Teacher burnout
- Increased school violence

For those reasons and more, we're exhausted and many of us are reconsidering our career choice. It doesn't help morale that education is under relentless scrutiny or that teachers continue to be lambasted in the headlines. We know our education system is in need of serious TLC, and I believe most of us are doing the very best with what we've got.

I see you, sweet educator, and you're drained. Exhausted at the *beginning* of the day, physically and mentally defeated by the bureaucratic bullshit that has taken precedence in your school. Adding insult to injury, your new building principal, the school board president's BFF who taught for three seconds two decades ago and hasn't been inside the classroom since, knows only what the board tells him about your day-to-day operations, yet there he is with his big plans and bigger paycheck, and you're on the verge of flipping a desk or sobbing in the faculty lounge or both because *no one hears you.* The negative vibes from work are seeping into your bloodstream, carrying contagions the whole way home. Your poor loved ones: They suffer the brunt of your exasperated wrath because, well, they can't fire you. The mounting dread as Sunday afternoon turns into Sunday evening is palpable; for, tomorrow, you'll drag yourself out of bed with a deflated heart and consider calling in sick (again), but eventually walk the green mile to your classroom and hope for a better day. But at this rate, it takes only one event, no matter how minor, to set the familiar downward spiral into motion once again.

Do you know why there's such an exodus from teaching? Because teaching is adulting on steroids. *We are responsible for people!* In a day and age when the rest of the world looks to us to replace a parental influence, no wonder so many of us are like, "Peace out!" How many other professions are responsible for churning out capable citizens? Talk about stress in the workplace.

But please hear me: *You* can make it better.

Stop rolling your eyes—I'm serious! All you've got to do is stop waiting for everyone else to make it better for you because

that

ain't

gon'

happen.

The power is within you.

Think: Why did you become a teacher in the first place? I've asked a plethora of teacher friends and family, as well as polled my Facebook community of some 60,000 people, and the majority has spoken: We became teachers because, in short, we are *"can people."* As in the verb form—you enjoy and excel at understanding and inspiring others. Do you even realize what a gift that is? *Because it is.* An individual who willingly stands before a room full of expectant minds and teaches, engages and challenges them—that is *"people-ing"* at its finest. So, why not get back to your roots and find ways to relate to your students that go beyond your day-to-day lesson plan? The kids without support at home won't suddenly have it, but they will have support from you, and that means something. To those kids, it just might mean everything.

But how?

Every district's circumstances and resources are different, and I'm just spitballing a few ideas here, but hopefully some of these speak to you.

Step Outside the Classroom

It's true, these ideas require more off-the-clock time, but they're an invaluable way to begin building that ever-important rapport with our students. During my first year of teaching, a high school junior I didn't even have in class, Uju, walked into my room and asked whether I would consider helping her start a step team and serve as its coach. When I asked, "How will I coach something I don't even know how to do?", Uju revised her question, replacing "coach" with "adviser," and I agreed to consider it, mostly so she would go away. By the end of the day, word of her request had spread, and handfuls of students popped into my classroom, begging me to "advise" their would-be step team. I noticed some of these were the same kids I'd been struggling to engage in class. Hmmm . . .

So began my love affair with stepping. I took my role as adviser seriously, advising against moves that were too, ahem, adult for school ("we do not twerk"), mitigated arguments—oh, so many arguments!—and laid down the law when necessary. Someone inevitably threatened to quit during every practice, and when tensions were especially high, I broke it down on the dance floor as a form of comic relief. Sweet, sweet Katie attempted (and failed) to teach me so many steps. I clapped when I should've stomped, stomped when I should've clapped. *Gah!* No wonder they always wanted to quit! *It was hard!* But I kept trying and we all kept laughing and it was all kinds of messy wonderful. Eventually, we got enough routines down that we were ready to show them off. The school went wild every time we performed at a pep rally, and that was enough to keep the team together.

Behind our success, trouble was brewing. Because step team hadn't been a preapproved club, there was no compensation for my extracurricular time. A few colleagues took umbrage with my choice to sponsor an unpaid activity, pressuring me to step down until it was written into our contract. I understood their perspective and the bigger picture, but I'd already begun reaping step-team-related rewards in my classroom. Pre–step team, many of the steppers had been doing next to nothing in class. Post–step team, the same students really started to shine: They volunteered to read in class, completed more homework and scored better on tests. For me, that was the biggest picture; I refused to quit.

Our time together at practice also opened doors for real talk about race and education and other things every school in America should be talking about but aren't. At the end of the season, I knew we had accomplished much more than a step team. The students must have felt the same because they awarded me my "Black Card."

At first, I was like, "What now?" Even writing about it today, I struggle with an explanation because all I did was treat them how I treat all my students, with the addition of my amazing dance moves of course. But Zante helped me understand:

> As a new teacher, we were [all] kind of nervous how you were going to handle a group of Black kids dancing and stepping to urban music. You sat back and observed, and then when you got more comfortable, you didn't play any games! You could've just let us practice and went about your business, but you actually made us [practice] until it sounded right. You made us dance until we were all in sync. And you made us care about our grades by making us stay eligible. You earned your Black Card because of your unconditional love and respect for us. You weren't scared to put us in our place and you let us be creative. I will always have a place in my heart for you.

I'm not crying, you're crying.

All I did was show up for them.

That is why I beg of you, fellow educator: Before you hang it up, try it out. I had nary a clue about stepping, but I signed on because I recognized the potential it held. From benefitting my students' learning to building relationships outside of the classroom, stepping outside of my comfort zone (see what I did there) was a win-win.

Is this crazy lady telling me to start a step team?

Yes. It's good exercise. Kidding! Just do something new.

Go, put yourself out there! Coach a sport, sponsor a club, mentor kids who need someone like you in their lives. Hint: If you bring food, they will come.

If you read all that and thought, "Sounds great in theory, but logistically I can't make it happen," no worries, I'm on it. Try some of these other ideas—when implemented correctly, they take anywhere from three to seven minutes. I totally made up those numbers, but only to prove these things are not time-consuming and you can do them before or during class time.

Stay in the Classroom, Just Think Outside the Box

Teachers understand that we can't expect students to learn if their basic needs aren't met. With very little effort, I'm sure you can list names of students you know don't eat breakfast before school or whose clothes are dirty or whose family life leaves a lot to be desired. That's why so many schools now provide students a solid foundation for learning, beginning with a free hot breakfast. We can't serve meals in our classrooms, but we can easily dish out compassion and grace. That's why I highly encourage teachers to do any or all these things regardless of your current situation or outlook. To echo my four-year-old daughter's glitter mantra: More is more.

Say hello: Greet your students as they enter the classroom. No, not just a nod from your desk; wait out in the hallway and speak to everyone as they arrive. Ask about last night's wrestling match, compliment a new haircut, check on a grandma who was ill last week. Making personal connections with your students takes only a little bit of time, and it makes a huge impact.

Run a two-minute drill: When my husband was young, he and his friends played pickup basketball with a youth pastor in a church gym. At the end of the game, the pastor, who recognized the opportunity in that precious time, used a fraction of it to impart religious lessons. Teachers can follow suit. Our two-minute drills can be thematic, tied to whatever we're reading in class, or universal messages geared toward specific age-groups: for younger kids, such topics as taking turns, sharing, being a good friend, peer pressure and sticking up for another student; for older grades, such topics as character, work ethic, integrity and honesty. These two-minute drills are perfect for injecting Real Talk into each day.

Pick one, any one!: I think a lot of teacher burnout stems from feeling like our efforts are fruitless. Let's change that by creating a tangible, feel-good goal that encompass the art of *people-ing*. Choose one kiddo and make his or her academic success your personal mission. How about the student who wants to come out to his parents? Or the girl who obviously admires you because she appears in your doorway in between every class? Ooh, ooh, how about the kid who continues to struggle with reading, but you can feel is on the verge of a breakthrough? Likely, as you're reading this, a specific face has already popped into your mind. Go to work tomorrow and seek out that face. Make a concerted effort to connect on a regular basis. If you see you're impacting just one student, you may feel compelled to stick around. Go! Get involved, show you care, and if that doesn't feed your soul, I'll reimburse you for this book.[1]

Kill 'em with kindness: On my first day at a new school, I had just finished introducing myself to the students and asked whether they had any questions. A sophomore girl who had been glaring at me the entire time I spoke raised her hand but didn't wait for me to call on her before blurting out, "I don't like new people." Inwardly, I was taken aback, but quickly scanned her classmates to find them rolling their eyes and scrunching up their noses in disgust at the girl's words. Something told me to treat her kindly. I shrugged and smiled, "That's okay; I'm not here to make friends. We'll just learn together." Within weeks, that child was following me around like a puppy dog because I hadn't immediately written her off. I found out ever since her father left, she feared everyone else would, too. To prevent herself from feeling vulnerable, this fifteen-year-old used sass and provocation to test the waters, trying to identify who she could count on and who she couldn't. It was obvious the other students hadn't passed her test, understandably not willing to be on the receiving end of her boldness, but it broke my heart anyway.

---

[1] fake news

The hardened façade our students construct as a means of protecting themselves can make it difficult to see their tender hearts behind it. We all need grace the most when we deserve it the least.

Celebrate the positive: When you see something good, share it! Call parents; send an email; send snail mail (everyone loves mail that isn't asking for money!); do what my amazing teacher pal Beth does and slap a Post-it note on students' desks when you catch them hard at work. Positivity begets positivity. It's science or something.

Cut tension with humor: When in doubt, laugh. Obviously, this advice depends on the situation, but if you have my brother's gift of recalling applicable movie quotes at just the right time, have at it. Otherwise, try to take more of the mess in stride. We do it in parenting, why not teaching?

Speak in the universal language of music: It's so easy to infuse music into learning! Play music as students enter the classroom; blast the *Rocky* theme song to get them pumped up for testing; dissect song lyrics for figurative language; have a celebratory soundtrack at the ready to acknowledge the positive as mentioned above! *throws confetti*

Don't Forget Your Colleagues: Don't you love being told you're doing a good job or that you're appreciated? Yeah, we all do. Put a note in a colleague's mailbox to let him know he's doing a kick-ass job; thank your principals for an insight-ful professional development series; seek out inspiration by observing your gifted fellow teachers at work in their class-rooms.

Schools need teachers like you. Don't stop wishing and working, but try not to get caught up in the things that haven't panned out the way you'd hoped. Instead, focus on putting more good out there. It'll help someone who needs it, maybe when you least expect it, and it'll surely make your heart happy. A happy teacher sticks around. Give it a try, will ya? Stick around.

Teacher Truth

Anyone who reheats last night's salmon in the faculty lounge microwave deserves lunch and bus duty for eternity.

part II

Every Day Feels
Like Monday

Teacher Tip

Practice your poker face for parent-teacher conference night. You're welcome.

Why Do I Kind of Hate This Job?

Originally, I went to college for a journalism degree. Naively, I believed journalists spent a lot of time with people, but quickly learned the chances of my being Oprah were slim and my job would likely have less to do with people and more to do with paper. An extrovert by nature, I felt isolated and deflated after one semester. The realization that a change was in order slowly dawned on me, but I wasn't quite mature enough to admit my mom had been right. Growing up, she always told me I'd make a great teacher, which is naturally why I chose to major in journalism. Teenagers are fun like that. But now I had no choice. If there was any chance of being passionate about my career, my teenaged self would have to swallow her pride and give Mom the satisfaction of being right all along. Swallow and switch I did, enrolling in the university's education program.

I instantly felt at home. The education courses focused on people, specifically young people who were figuring out how to be grown people. I was ecstatic to be a part of their journey. Teaching meant a chance to make a difference, to really impact the future, and almost twenty years later, I feel the same affection and passion for my career as I did when I started.

That said, I'd be a lying liar if I didn't admit there are parts of the job that make me want to ram a sharpened #2 through my eye socket.

And you know the sick irony of it all? It's mostly the people who make me crazy! The same people I longed to surround myself with—the ones I changed the trajectory of my career to include—they're a pain in my whole ass. And unlike most other professionals, a teacher's success or failure is determined by none other than those pains! We can't control their behavior or their efforts, yet a teacher's day—maybe even entire career—is at the mercy of So. Many. People.

One group is, of course, the students. For example, the students I refer to as the "indifferent brains" are certainly eye-stab worthy. There's nothing worse than apathetic, capable teenagers already filled to the gills with premature jaded cynicism, the likes of which have turned them into academic sloths. They answer questions with shoulder shrugs and respond to essay prompts with question marks and on the rare occasion they do speak, it's nothing more than a mumbled passive-aggressive insult, and OMG, I can feel my blood pressure rising right this very minute. I will always prefer a student who holds my brain cells hostage with an essay so jacked up with convoluted ramblings that the only reasonable feedback I can muster is, "What in the actual hell are you talking about?" I celebrate this student! I slow clap his garbage essay. Why? Because at least he cared enough to turn in something.

Similar in variety to the IDGAF[1] students are the ones who sit in the very back of the room and make eye contact with you as they do the exact opposite of what you've just asked the class to do. The ones who, after you've introduced a new project, raise their hand to ask, "When will I ever need to know this in real life?" These students aspire only to ruffle feathers and love nothing more than interrupting anything that resembles harmonious learning. Their objective to drag others down with their sinking ship makes them twice as infuriating as their quiet, lazy counterparts. Class runs smoother when these distracting buttholes aren't there, which is why teachers do a happy dance when we find them on the absentee bulletin.

A more complex version of distracting students is the thankfully small group who just can't leave well enough alone. These are the students who have no qualms about starting fights over petty things that most other humans could let slide. I refer to these students as "Destroyers," since the day a few of them literally shattered my classroom window. Story time:

I'd spent about 200 of my own dollars creating a reading nook in a corner of my very first classroom. There were beanbag chairs, floor lamps, an area rug; a bookcase boasting more new young adult titles than our school library! Books

---

[1] I don't give a fuck

of poetry, autobiographical essays from pop culture icons, Harry Potter and more filled the shelves. I was hyped about the space and ready to introduce students to the future love of their lives: reading!

Not even a week later, two Destroyers got into a fight because one of them looked at the other crooked or something stupid. Punches started in the hallway and ended when Boy A threw Boy B through my classroom window, destroying the precious reading nook that lay beneath it. I was grateful Boy B's book bag led the charge on the window, as it was the only true victim of the spraying glass. I also realized I was lucky I hadn't been standing two feet closer. Had I taken just a few steps toward the door, I would've resembled the beanbag chairs: sliced and scarred by jagged shards.

By day's end, all debris had been removed, the classroom window temporarily covered with cardboard. Because they were indiscriminately maimed with glass remnants, the chairs, rug and most of the books had to be thrown away. All that remained of the reading nook were my good intentions, the road to my classroom apparently paved with them. This incident prompted my first professional gut-check; I left school that day considering the possibility that I might actually hate my job.

Not all students are maddening year-round or willingly destroy school property on the regular. This sounds great in theory, but believe you me, they make up for it during the last month of school. Expert opinion (mine) believes these students are affected by ASS, Annual Student Shutdown.

When the end of the school year is nigh, ASS kicks laziness into high gear. Students justify their ridiculous behavior or craptastic grades with *"The year is basically over anyway,"* and it is then that I feel compelled to duct-tape them to the wall, staple their eyelids to their foreheads and force them to watch my interpretative dance of Shakespeare's classics.

It's a completely different story when a kid's home life is what's interfering with the school day. Seemingly increasing in both severity and frequency, the heartbreaking conditions that affect far too many of our students cause teachers a different kind of frustration: helplessness. We see the problem—family dynamics, addiction, homelessness—but have no power to fix it. We are so consumed with worry, struggling to strike a reasonable balance between parenting them and educating them, that at the end of the school day, we bring these kids home with us. They're on our minds at the dinner table, serving as a catalyst to remind our own children how very lucky they are. They're with us at bedtime when all we want to do is turn off our brains. They're at the center of our lesson planning as we take great pains to avoid triggering topics and content. This shit isn't Vegas: What happens at home, does *not* stay at home. Kids carry their heavy burdens to class in the form of bloodshot, exhausted eyes; nonexistent academic drive; hungry bellies; and defiant, sometimes explosive tempers. Add unaddressed mental health issues to the mix, and we've got some downright tragic and dangerous situations in our schools.

Edgar Allan Poe's short story "The Cask of Amontillado" once triggered a student in my junior English class. Admittedly, the story is kind of macabre, ending with the protagonist buried alive behind a wall, but it's also a high-interest story for high school kids . . . usually. I can still see his sobbing six-foot, two-inch frame dwarfing the desk in which he sat, an unsettling contrast. After running a mental marathon trying to decide the best course of action, I ultimately opted to put my hand gently on his shoulder, intending to soothe him while simultaneously attempting to continue the lesson. Abruptly, he bucked like a stallion trying to throw off its rider and in two long strides was out the classroom door and gone.

I stood there speechless, tears stinging my eyes. Everyone looked at me, expecting an explanation. I was thankful when a boy interrupted the stunned silence with "He does that sometimes," and we went back to the story. Similar scenarios with this student repeated several times over the course of the year, careening between maniacal and erratic behavior to sudden emotional outbursts, all of which led him to leave or be escorted from the class. The school psychologist would later unofficially diagnose the student with bipolar disorder, urging his parents to seek professional guidance and treatment, neither of which ever happened. Our class was always on pins and needles when he was there. His unpredictable, unaddressed behavior made us uneasy and I felt especially useless because there was nothing I could do to help him. No one could control the circumstances that affected us all.

Teachers expect and accept that we will handle a certain level of unbecoming conduct from our students as part of the job. We also anticipate that less than ideal circumstances will stand between us and our students. But what I personally didn't anticipate was how fellow educators would get under my skin! In my first department meeting at a new school, I proposed we introduce a new novel to the curriculum, reasoning the content was more relevant and engaging for students. I saw a doubtful look cross one colleague's face, but she didn't say anything. Until, that is, she cornered me in the hall later that day, hissing like an angry parent scolding her insolent child. She then gave me the worst reason in the world for not agreeing to the new title: "I've been teaching the same books for almost thirty years, and you're not going to swoop in here and change everything!" She wagged her finger at me as she reminded me of my place in the pecking order. I rolled my eyes and wished she would just retire already.

I like to know what I'm working with up front, so I was at least grateful my gem of a new coworker had shown her true colors right away. I tried giving her the benefit of the doubt, thinking maybe she worked better with students and was amazing in the classroom. That didn't turn out to be the case. In fact, it became obvious that this woman was our department's weakest link. Her instructional style could best be summed up as "worksheets from 1950." She never volunteered for anything or tried her hand at new projects, and the rest of us avoided collaborating with her because we knew the brunt of the work would be ours. Maybe this teacher had been through the ringer too many times with administrators or was suffering from the professional fatigue that has become synonymous with teaching and that's why she was so rigid.

Whatever the case, at the end of the day, her students were getting the short end of the stick and that irked me. She wasn't a team player, but at least she waved her "nope" flag where the rest of us could see. Other colleagues are much sneakier when it comes to their nope.

Nowhere are these shifty teachers more prominent than when we work together across the disciplines. My English department once teamed up with the history and math departments on a fantastic cross-curricular project. It became very evident a select few of us were carrying everyone else, as we scheduled the library time, created the rubrics and were the only ones answering the students' incessant questions. When we agreed to do the project, it was because we had all seen the value in it, but it became clear that some of the teachers didn't necessarily see the strength in numbers, but a chance to hide among the numbers. Literally. Like, I found a bunch of them hiding in an empty classroom with the lights off and door closed.

We're all stretched thin, I get it. But to unapologetically bail in the middle of the project means the rest of us double up on responsibilities and that's a bush league move.

Speaking of bush league, dare I crack open a case on administrators? I've worked with a few who are academic soldiers on the front lines of educational reform, inspiring necessary change for all students. They lead by example, have the kids' best interest at heart and successfully collaborate with teachers and other educators to ensure we're all invested in the same goal. I've also worked with the other side of the coin, where the administrators are, shall we say, less effective. The overarching problem with these principals is they are professional yes-men controlled by the superintendent's puppet strings. They resist the change schools need because it means their job security. Some may say, "Who can blame them?" I can. Over a period of years, one such complacent administrator in a local district drew vast and continuous concerns and complaints from his staff and community. When the superintendent finally stepped in, it wasn't to improve the principal's professional conduct as would happen to a teacher with a performance plan, additional training, extra support, et cetera. Nope, the superintendent simply transferred the principal to another building. Instead of solving the problem, he moved it, forcing another group of teachers and students to deal with it. Bush. League.

Another of my former principals was supposed to observe all us new teachers at least three times during our first year, fulfilling a requirement of our teaching contract. Dude just wouldn't show up! This happened to my colleagues and me numerous times. Not only did it waste our time to plan for an observation that never came, but we also feared how it would reflect in our permanent file. Because formal observation notes would be a determining factor of our earned tenure, we believed our concerns were justified. However, when we inquired about this, our principal suggested we "worry about what's important." So, I guess only administrators are allowed to concern themselves with job security.

As exasperating as that principal was, I'd rather a no-show than one who micromanages our every decision. We all understand educational stakes and tensions are especially high right now, but when teachers are given limited control over our classrooms, we get the feeling someone's trying to tell us we're incompetent. What's more is the micromanager has so much on his plate, he's usually working under pressure and strict deadlines. Guess who suffers from the trickle-down of said pressure and deadlines?

Look, I'd never want to be a principal today. They're the middle Russian nesting doll in the educational hierarchy, dealing with so much more than I'm capable of handling without being arrested. As the face of our schools, they contend with unreasonable parents and angry community members and constantly have the higher-ups breathing down their necks. All I'm saying is that some of them, along with some of our students and teachers, suck. That's a fair assessment, right?

The frustrating parts of our job can feel a lot like a wall of concrete, trapping us for life like one of Poe's characters. There's good news to be had, though. Take a stroll through the heart of any city and you'll likely find flowers blooming through cracks in the concrete, stretching toward the sun. They're not just surviving—they're flourishing in spite of their conditions. They exhibit the kind of fortitude and "I've got this" attitude that teachers know so well. A fraction of the people we deal with can make or break us, but there are so many others who are worth stretching for. And here's the thing about working with people in general: They make it so no day looks the same. They keep us on our toes, learning and excited, which is one of my favorite parts of the job.

So, on days when that #2 pencil starts looking mighty tempting, try to remember: We didn't get into teaching to work with paper. We might hate our job today, but tomorrow is a mulligan. A shot at a do-over, a second chance. Tomorrow, a student will repeat our classroom mantra "I will not give up" unprompted and double down on that hard math problem. Come tomorrow, the kid who had been aloof will meet your eye and smile. Maybe mañana, the senior no one thought would make it will earn his high school diploma. Get through today because tomorrow, you'll fall in love with teaching, and the people it involves, all over again.

Meeting the Tree

You know the saying "The apple doesn't fall far from the tree"? Teachers are in the unique position to witness said fall firsthand.

Every year at parent-teacher conferences, we are introduced to the individuals responsible for the ~~apples'~~ students' predominate qualities. Sometimes we get lucky and those qualities include an amazing work ethic, a gift for writing or a talent for math, a passion for learning or a fantastic sense of humor.

Other times, we are brought face-to-face with the reason that we fantasize about leaving our jobs. Students who think the world should accommodate them, who are entitled and combative, certainly learn their behavior from someone. Enter: the tree. While the trees differ in severity and demeanor, they all share one distinguishing characteristic: They blame you, not their kid.

These trees reveal their crazy in different ways, but the following scenarios are commonplace during parent-teacher conferences:

Weeping Willow: This tree acts shocked upon hearing about their child's behavior or academic performance. They proclaim harsher than necessary consequences will be implemented "the second we get home." They assume their lip service in front of an audience has convinced everyone they will actually address these issues. Nothing will change.

Burning Bush: This tree comes in hot, yelling about things their special snowflake has claimed are going on in the classroom and with our grading system. We can't get a word in edgewise as the tree repeatedly makes their point, which is always: "My kid is right, you are wrong."

Poison Oak: This tree begins the conference laid-back, asking questions that also kinda sorta sound like allegations, and once they have obtained what they consider enough "incriminating evidence," throws it back in our face, calling us names like unfair/unprofessional/inexperienced/a sack of dog shit. It's then we realize they aren't here for a conference so much as a confrontation.

Let's explore these kinds of trees as to better understand their apples, shall we?

The Weeping Willow

Carlos was a freshman, always in trouble for something. His behavior wasn't horrendous; I'd categorize it as annoying. He made noises while I was teaching, interrupted other students and couldn't keep his hands to himself. He was basically a puppy growing into his paws, who meant no harm, but at the same time, *OMG, someone crate him.*

I'd been considering contacting his mom when, conveniently, I ran into her one afternoon as she was picking up Carlos from school. As she and Carlos followed me into my classroom, she hissed the consequences he would endure for his behavior.

Making a conscious effort to "sandwich" the conversation—which is teacher speak for start with a positive, slip in the negative and end on another positive—I began by commending him for being active during class discussions.

Me: I love that Carlos wants to participate in class . . .

Then, slipped in the negative . . .

. . . but he needs to wait his turn and stop interrupting—

Her: You're not telling me anything I don't know! That boy never stops talking at home! Just yesterday he . . .

Me: *feigned interest while she talked over me for another 10 minutes*

And that's how our entire conversation went. Each of my sentences was punctuated with an example of her equal aggravations at home.

Then, I attempted to delicately tell her Carlos is a bit handsy in class, punching other students in the arm or pretending to tackle his cousin in the hall. To my horror, she reeled around and smacked him upside the back of the head. "Even little kids know to keep their hands to themselves! What is wrong with you?"

Apple, meet tree.

The Burning Bush

These "Oh no, you di'n't" trees refuse to accept responsibility for their kids' indiscretions because, in their bubble world, there are no indiscretions to speak of. Many of the tree's sentences begin with "My child said" or "My child would never." Forget the fact that we're the adult or that we have how many years of experience dealing with kids. We are wrong. We are dumb. We know nothing. Take, for instance, Julie.

Julie just couldn't seem to remember to turn in her essays, despite my communicating due dates via a course schedule, the Remind app, text messages, heads-up emails, smoke signals in the sky, et cetera. Poor Julie continually failed to meet deadlines, therefore, failing her assignments. Do you know what happens when Burning Bush apples earn an F? If you guessed that their parent gets all up in your face, spit-yelling, you are correct!

It didn't matter that I showed Julie's parents the schedules and reminders or simply stated it was Julie's responsibility to know the due dates; they started in on me about how I demand too much of the students, how technology fails them and how Julie never earned a grade lower than a B before my class. Fighting the urge to counter with, "There's a first time for everything," I offered Julie an extension: She had two more days.

When the time came, Julie turned in a mostly plagia-rized essay, opening a whole new can of worms. Her parents demanded a sit-down with our principal and department chair, insisting I didn't understand the difference between plagiarizing an essay and including research in an essay. They requested a change of teachers because I was "unfairly targeting their student," and as a result, Julie couldn't achieve academic success. I silently prayed my principal would just put the kid in a different class, but since he was never one to negotiate with crazy, the request was denied. Julie basically stopped working, stopped completing homework and began missing a lot of school. This was, of course, also my fault.

This was years ago, but I did recently hear Julie is having a hard time holding down a job today. *Shocking.*

The Poison Oak

While Julie and her parents are more aggressive in their efforts to avoid accountability, the Poison Oak apple and tree are more surreptitious in their stance. Rather than participating in class or bothering to pay attention to the content, the Poison Oak apple sits like a lump in his desk, silently observing what he perceives to be his teachers' shortcomings, and then goes home to share his findings with his tree. And let's be clear about those shortcomings; they include anything the student doesn't like but, for the sake of learning, is expected to do. The Poison Oak apple prefers more kinesthetic activities, but today's lesson requires notetaking? Strike one. He doesn't feel confident with short-answer essays? Strike two. He is offended by authority? Strike three.

My first experience with this kind of student and his parents took me by surprise, which makes sense since that's the Poison Oak way. Neither Poison Oak apple Pat nor his parents had ever voiced their concerns to me, so I was understandably perplexed the day I was called into my principal's office to find Mr. and Mrs. Poison Oak waiting for me. For people who never spoke directly to me, they sure did seem to know a lot about me and my class! Dad literally opened a notebook filled with anecdotal evidence that, according to their son, proved I was an incompetent educator. I sat there quietly as he advised me on how I should have addressed certain issues, comparing his experiences in corporate America to "what it is teachers do." When it came time to discuss his son's grades, though, there was no excuse or scapegoat left:

Poison Oak: On November ninth, you gave my son a zero on his independent novel project.

Me: Correct.

Poison Oak: Why is that?

Me: He didn't turn it in.

The conversation continued in much of the same manner, with the Poison Oak parents' inquisition inadvertently revealing their son's lack of effort as the real reason for the meeting. Perhaps a different kind of parent would have realized their ownership in the situation, but we know that's not how Poison Oaks roll.

By the end of the meeting, I had been instructed to email the Poison Oak parents any time their son didn't turn in an assignment or earned a failing grade. My polite reminder that our gradebooks were online for their convenience was ignored, and I spent the rest of that school year sending emails that never received responses.

....

As with most things in teaching, there's a beautiful silver lining I need you to know about: For every diseased, wilted tree, there are twice as many mighty spruces and blooming magnolias. Incredible parents and fantastic students who understand and appreciate teachers far outnumber the others. You'll know these parents by the way they support our efforts to educate their child, trusting that we're all on the same team. They may reach out in gratitude or gift you with platters of cookies during the holidays. Or they may simply agree when we tell them, "Your kid can do better." You'll recognize their students by their earnest attempts in class. These parents and kids are the ones we stick around for, the ones that make this job worth it. So, I beg of you: Don't miss the forest for the trees.

Zip It, Lock It, Put It in Your Pocket: What Teachers Say vs. What We Mean

When my now ten-year-old son finished preschool, he brought home a nugget of wisdom I've used ever since: "Zip it, lock it, put it in your pocket." An adorable rhyme that's easy to remember, it's a kid-friendly way of saying shut your face hole. Applicable across generations and relating to a wide variety of topics, this phrase is the gift that keeps on giving.

Because educators walk a tightrope of respectability narrower than most, we're used to "zipping it" more than the average employee, lest we get ourselves into trouble. I get it, though. No one wants their kid to have the teacher who freely drops F-bombs at the grocery store or who verbally annihilates a student for making a mistake in class. While other careers don't carry as much weight in this respect, the collision of teachers' public and personal personas is a well-known hazard of the job. Educators take a much more delicate approach when problem-solving and communicating.

But we have limits, too.

There have been plenty of times we've wanted to shout, "You're killin' me, Smalls!" and storm off, letting the student who asked the very question we just answered seventeen times fend for himself. If we had a dollar for every time we fought the urge to yell, "We are all now dumber for having listened to you!" during a faculty meeting, we'd rival Beyoncé's net worth. The fact that we possess the willpower that keeps us from laughing in a parent's face when she tells us her son has always been an A student before he had our class proves that teachers are superhuman. But I warn you: Just because we're zipping it, doesn't mean we're not thinking it.

Professional decorum may disagree, but I'm sharing a sneak peek inside an educator's brain so you can get a whiff of what's going on behind the scenes.

When a parent insists the 36 assignments her child turned in on the last day of school be graded immediately to determine if he passed . . .

What teachers think: Couldn't return my calls or emails all year, but *now* you care?! Sure, I'll get right on your superreasonable request! *puts student's 36 assignments at very bottom of to-do list*

What teachers say: I appreciate your concern and will try my hardest to get these graded.

When a student who has earned a 5 percent for the entire marking period asks for extra credit, citing "I'm not good at meeting deadlines" as justification . . .
What teachers think: I see you're not very good at math, either.
What teachers say: It's great to see you're motivated!

When the school counselor asks to speak to your class about the new antibullying campaign and gives you zero notice . . .
What teachers think: *Awesome!* I just love unexpected interruptions and a blatant disregard for my time.
What teachers say: Sure thing. We'll make it work.

When a parent sees you at a restaurant and asks to discuss his student's progress in your class . . .
What teachers think: Is nothing sacred?! Also, do I have spinach in my teeth? OMG, does he know this is my third glass of wine?
What teachers say: *whatever will make him go away the fastest*

When a colleague repeatedly "drops in" on your plan period . . .
What teachers think: I just cannot with this. Do you not

see me avoiding eye contact? *I am busy!*

What teachers say: Mmmhmm. I know, right? Fascinating. Ya don't say?!

When the administration instructs you to create a monthly calendar with assignments and due dates for a student who's too lazy to do it for himself . . .

What teachers think: Excellent! I think enabling this kid to be as useless as possible has success written all over it.

What teachers say: I'm on it.

A student's grades and attendance keep him from being eligible for the National Honors Society, but his pushy parents insist he's NHS material. To avoid conflict with the family, your principal demands you, the NHS sponsor, let the student join. . . .

What teachers think: Are you fucking kidding me?

What teachers say: If that's what you think is best, that's what I'll do.

When a parent says her child would never cheat on a test . . .

What teachers think: They said the *Titanic* was unsinkable and we all know how that turned out.

What teachers say: *clutches imaginary pearls* I was just as surprised as you!

Your principal hasn't formally observed you in more than a decade! But today he tells you to create a lesson plan implementing the new technology he introduced at last week's in-service, and that he'll be observing you next Monday. . . .

What teachers think: Sure, that's legal and best practice. The fact that you're employed makes me nauseous.

What teachers say: I'll do my best.

When an absent student returns and asks, "Did we do anything while I was out?" . . .

What teachers think: Why would I waste time teaching if *you're* not here?! We sat and stared at one another instead.

What teachers say: Please check the absent folder/file for notes, assignments and updates, as per usual policy.

It's helpful to keep a stack of these "school-appropriate" comebacks handy for the days we encounter unusually high volumes of ridiculousness that render our ability to react like upstanding educators useless. Think of these educational comebacks as a teacher's version of *Cards Against Humanity*, but instead of hilariously obscene options, we have universally accepted and politically correct responses at our fingertips.

Teacher Tip

Choose your ringtone carefully. There will come a day you forget to put your phone on SILENT, and you don't want to be the teacher known for LMFAO's "Sexy and I Know It."

Secret Shortcuts
and Level-Up Partners
for Teachers

The younger the students, the more resourceful the educators are, and after raising three small humans of my own, I now understand this brand of ingenuity is born out of necessity. The simplest task is made ten times more difficult when little kids are involved. By this logic, getting a class of 25 kindergarteners to line up for a bathroom break requires the same energy and time as running a half marathon. I raise my cup of thrice reheated coffee to you, elementary school teachers!

Regardless of what grade we teach, teachers are all looking for better, faster, more efficient ways to do things and this, too, is out of necessity. With everything we're expected to accomplish in a single school day, every second counts, which is probably why so many Pinterest boards are dedicated to teaching hacks and shortcuts. No offense, Pinterest, but I'm coming to you solely for the low-carb cocktail recipes; I already have access to the best "teaching hacks" out there, and they don't require me to save empty toilet paper rolls for art projects. I'm talking about my colleagues, of course!

Valuable beyond the scope of their regular duties, these coworkers are delightful little surprises wrapped up in secretaries and biology teachers and custodians. Serving more than one purpose with equal efficiency, these talented professionals pull double duty, making the school day run that much smoother for everyone. Allow me to introduce you to the unsung heroes in your building:

Ingenuity Genius: This is your modern-day MacGyver, able to fend for himself in the Arctic and rig your SMART board with the same sure-handedness. Ingenuity Geniuses are often part of the maintenance staff, but if you work with a teacher who somehow manages to fund field trips on a next-to-nothing budget or who continually finds businesses to donate baked goods and drinks for end-of-the-year picnics, that's your resident Genius.

Red: Named after Morgan Freeman's character in the movie version of *The Shawshank Redemption*, Red is the getter of all things. This is your person for finding extra copies of novels and procuring additional funds to replace classroom supplies, and who has long been suspected of secretly owning Teachers Pay Teachers because of his access to never-ending lesson materials. You'll know your Red by the case of beer someone is always putting in his trunk in appreciation for his contributions.

Local Historian: Your school's Local Historian is likely the secretary who's been around the longest or the person who references the principal from three decades ago. These administrative wonders can recall dates and student names everyone else has long forgotten, not to mention list an entire family tree at the drop of a hat. Can't get in touch with a student's parent? Tell your Local Historian and you're guaranteed a list of grandparents, aunts, neighbors, church friends and third cousins will be in your inbox by the end of the day.

Building Tech Guru: These days, most every district has a technology supervisor, a person committed to implementing and supporting technology in our schools. This person is invaluable, which also means he's hella hard to get ahold of. Therefore, our most immediate technology woes are referred to our Building Tech Guru. This is the person who can help troubleshoot a connection to the server and also rescue those bachelor party pictures that were accidentally uploaded to the school's cloud. Oooopsie. Wondering who your in-house Guru is? Just listen for the name everyone yells when they're having Wi-Fi issues.

Pseudo-Parent: Look no further than your department chair to find your Pseudo-Parent. These professionals are sources of instructional knowledge who double as a soothing maternal presence, drawing from years of experience to talk you off the ledge and put bad days into perspective. Your Pseudo-Parent has been through the peaks and valleys of education and has likely adopted the motto "No sense in stressing over what we can't control." This person usually has candy hidden in a desk drawer and never forgets a birthday.

Mouthpiece: Perhaps your union president or the longest tenured teacher, every school's Mouthpiece is brave enough to say what the rest of us only think. They willingly go to bat for us and fight for our contracts, and miraculously, no one in administration messes with the Mouthpiece. We all aspire to arrive at this place in our career.

Work Spouse: This is your go-to person for all emotional things. Need to cry after a frustrating day of standardized testing? Work Spouse. Want to share the hilariously inappropriate thing your student said during class? Work Spouse. Have tea to spill (that's student-speak for having gossip to share) about that crazy PTA president? Work Spouse. Whoever's laughing at the same dumb jokes or recognizes *Billy Madison* as the finest film about education is your Work Spouse. Or maybe that's just mine?

The Fixer: There are several people on your maintenance staff, but only one of them is the Fixer. Here's how to properly identify yours: Wait until the middle of winter when your classroom heater is blowing cold air or, conversely, the middle of May when it's blasting hot dragon breath. Ask everyone in the maintenance department to adjust the temperature accordingly. The one who waltzes in, bangs on it with his fist and actually fixes it is officially your Fixer.

The Baker: If you don't celebrate and commiserate school successes and setbacks with baked goods, then you're a better person than I. A good chocolate chip cookie has been known to buoy me through standardized testing season and, therefore, has earned a special place in my teaching repertoire. Find your Baker and you'll uncover the person whose culinary side hustle gifts cakes for your kids' birthdays, trays of holiday cookies and delicious just-because treats on a random Tuesday. Whoever brings in homemade yummies for department meetings is your internal baker.

Principal's Pet: You missed that thing your principal announced at the last staff meeting because you and your Work Spouse were texting *Billy Madison* quotes back and forth. Fortunately, the resident Principal's Pet didn't miss a word and you can rely on him to fill you in. Nothing's easier than spotting your building's Pet; he's the only one taking notes at the meetings.

Across-the-Hall Friend: The only person physically capable of assisting your unexpected restroom needs, the Across-the-Hall Friend is positioned exactly at the halfway point between your classroom and hers, meaning she can keep an eye on both sets of students while you handle your bathroom bidness. No words can adequately express our gratitude for this friend.

Sixth Sense: I like to spy on my students whenever possible. It gives me a good idea of how they spend their time, with whom they spend it and alerts me to any unsavory extracurricular activities. Because I physically can't be everywhere at once (a detail I never share with students), I rely on a second set of eyes for my stealthy detective work. I like me a good bus driver or librarian, but anyone out of the classroom setting will do. Once I've collected all necessary information and subsequently addressed it with students, they assume I have a Sixth Sense and I take full credit for being the knower of all things.

These versatile, multifaceted men and women are better than any Dollar Store hack or instructional shortcut. They come through in the clutch every time, adding substance and heart to our school days. Because most of their contributions are behind the scenes, they likely don't get the recognition they deserve, which is why it can be difficult to identify them. So, here's a hack for your hack, a shortcut for your shortcut: If you need to know who your school's internal *anything* is, ask your Principal's Pet. He has a hierarchy of who's who laminated in a binder hidden on a shelf in his classroom.

The Month of May
Can Go Straight
to Hell

Every profession has its peaks and valleys, triumphs and challenges. But I don't think any other is as severely compromised by one month out of the year as teaching.

We all have seasons that are busier than others. My professional photographer pal disappears every year from June through September during the height of wedding season. The men and women in charge of road prep and snow removal 'round these western Pennsylvanian parts are used to working crazy hours in the winter months. I imagine labor and delivery nurses are extra busy every year around November 14 because of the people who got extra busy on February 14! Ha!

Wait. My birthday is November 14. Ewww, I no longer want to talk about this.

I have a point: If you're in education, please stand and testify that our valleys and challenges and busy schedules all collide in the month of May.

September is a new beginning, full of possibility and promise. Students are excited to see friends and show off their new kicks, while teachers are rejuvenated, their reservoirs of energy and patience having been restored over the summer. Floors are clean, things are in their place and smiling faces fill hallways and classrooms.

October is fairly calm with the exception of Halloween. Elementary school teachers dread it because of the chaos and sugar, while we secondary teachers are always on high alert for that one student who pushes the envelope with his costume. Once during a school Halloween parade, a senior wore regular street clothes and a saucepot on his head. Took me a minute before I realized he was dressed as a "pot head." Sigh. I'd be cool with Halloween if everyone would just give me their chocolate and not be stupid, but alas, 'tis never the case. Although it is only one day of the whole month, making the rest of October easy-peasy.

November hits and everyone is ready for a breather. Both school districts and the calendar have taken proactive measures to accommodate us: parent-teacher conferences, professional development days and Thanksgiving provide a much-needed reprieve from the daily grind. We head into December with high spirits.

December is a celebratory month because of the holidays, but mostly because we see a light at the end of the tunnel in the form of an extended vacation from school. *Can I get an "Amen"?* The shorter, colder days also allow us to hibernate after school, so once the last bell rings, we're going home and not leaving until morning.

January feels fresh like September, with an extra layer of resolve added to it. Because we're not in school for the full month, January seems very doable. And then comes . . .

Farch. February + March = a lifetime and is generally when I begin reconsidering my career path. Even in warmer climates where never-ending gunmetal skies and depressing freezing temperatures don't exist, there are no major holidays to look forward to. Farch drags ooooooonnnnn and ooooooonnnnn. By March 31, I have cashed in a mental health day or three and am ready to relocate to the Cayman Islands. That said, these months are very much by the book with limited outside distractions interrupting class time, so even though they're long, they're at least productive.

April is the resurrection. Of testing, of course. Instruction is compromised because we have to be test-focused, but the silver lining is spring break. Bless this break. Enjoy this break. Savor every second of this break. Because once we turn the calendar, you will neither enjoy nor savor anything until the last day of school. Because, May.

Oh, May. How do I hate thee? Let me count thy ways. . . .

First of all, May is an imposter. With hues of bright blue once again painting the sky, cornflowers dotting hillsides and brilliant sunshine warming the earth, May looks idyllic. On the outside, it exudes serenity and peace, but one look inside a school and you'll soon find the month is nothing but chaos. May is comprised of approximately 67 days with an average of eighteen hours per day, and thanks to the extended daylight, outside activities last even longer. Oh, and those activities? Whether indoor or out, they all take place in May. All of them. Field trips, field days, Teacher Appreciation Week, senior nights, banquets, concerts, prom, Nurse's Day, IEP (individualized education plan) meetings, showcases, Memorial Day, fund-raisers, final exams, junior Olympics, fitness tests, games, contests, ceremonies, graduation, assemblies, end-of-school awards and who could forget finalizing then refinalizing grades at the eleventh hour because come May, extra credit becomes the same as regular credit. Weeeeee! Any semblance of a normal school day is obliterated by the unending barrage of May activities and responsibilities.

Secondly, May turns classrooms into dens of oppressive heat.

Before we discuss this further, let's deodorize all the middle schoolers in our lives. Please and thank you.

Moving on. It's so swampy in our classrooms that everyone sweats through their clothes before ten a.m. My greasy hair is drenched and piled on top of my head in a bun that says, "I've given up." I can't stop wiping my chin with the back of my hand, causing a colony of sweat pimples to set up shop there until July. I also can't chug ice water like any other person who's overheating because then I'll pee every 30 minutes, and we all know teachers don't have that luxury. The heat is suffocating and exacerbates our itchy eyes and runny noses thanks to another gift of May: allergies. Students are miserable and can barely stay awake while teachers are grasping at straws trying to stick to the curriculum despite the incessant interruptions and sneezing. If there's any hope of putting something new in a kid's brain, it must be presented with jazz hands via a costumed Broadway show or another equally dramatic medium. I've considered introducing a new lesson atop an elephant, but I've heard that can be expensive, and I'm a teacher, thus broke.

Lastly, ghosts of children from yesteryear, also known as first semester, have been known to reappear in May. Kids we haven't seen in months materialize like truant apparitions, asking the age-old question, "Can I do extra credit to pass?" Some of us are prepared for this request, years of experience having taught us to keep a stack of assignments at the ready for this very purpose. We hand over the assignments and exchange a knowing look with the student, a silent acknowledgment that we both know those assignments, much like all the others, will never be seen again.

Other teachers use this opportunity to practice our "This Is Not How the World Works" speech, explaining the way to bring up grades is to do the work when it is assigned. The word *extra* means "in addition to," and because the regular work wasn't completed, extra credit doesn't even exist in their world. Our words fall on deaf ears, but still: Bye, Felicia.

Some of us entertain the idea of extra credit if other requirements are met first, namely a meeting with the student's parents. This rarely happens, though, because meeting with parents would mean the student has to come clean about how they pissed away the entire year. Instead they focus on intercepting their report card. We will hear from the parents when they call the school to ask why their student is in the same grade next year.

A small percentage of us will be visited by adult apparitions who have broken under the weight of May's stress and temptation. These administrators, fellow teachers, coaches and guidance counselors have all been afflicted with May-itis. This disease impairs professional neurological function and causes otherwise intelligent adults to interpret the calendar changing as the go-ahead to lower academic standards. Like my Apple watch giving me credit for standing, May suddenly makes it seem reasonable to award points for showing up. Have we fallen so far from grace, people? All Mays point to yes.

There's an added level of fuckery for teachers who have children of our own. Like it's not bad enough that the month ravages routine and efficiency in schools, but teacher-parents are doubly whooped. Not only are we fighting an uphill battle in our classrooms, but the war doesn't end with the final bell of the day. Oh, no. All those activities that have been interrupting the workday follow us home like a flea-infested puppy that will inevitably poop on the floor. We survive this time of the year on a wing, prayer and fast-food drive-throughs, silently hoping it'll rain so our kid's game will be canceled.

It is no coincidence "may" makes up words like *mayhem*, *mayday* and *dismay*. There is simply no escaping the over-scheduled exhaustion and chaos. But here's a tried-and-true tip I've used to survive this Dumpster fire of a month: Stop striving for that elusive work-life balance. It doesn't exist in

May, and the sooner we admit it, the better. Lunches will be eaten standing up, we'll make twice as many decisions than normal and proverbial fires will continue popping up that require our immediate attention. As such, our already limited social lives will take a back seat until at least mid-June, and I recommend we make peace with the fact that from now until the end of the year, teachers will be coming to school looking like zombies from *The Walking Dead*. It's fine. Everything is fine.

Teacher Tip

Dear educator, you will do amazing things.

You will move mountains and impact lives and inspire change.

Just not on the weekend. Take a break; you deserve it.

Things Every Teacher Needs

Have you ever wondered how different public education could be if our country perceived it to be as important as, say, professional sports? Imagine the possibilities if schools were equipped with all the bells and whistles like state-of-the-art arenas and sports complexes or if communities rallied 'round their learners the way they do their athletes. Wrap your brain around all that teachers could accomplish if everything they needed was at their fingertips. These are the things I fantasize about and yes, I, too, feel bad for my husband.

I salute professional basketball player LeBron James for making a top-of-the-line education available for students in his hometown of Akron, Ohio, though I don't look for him or his fellow athletes to fund every public school, so I'm taking matters into my own hands. Someone call Bill Gates or Tom Brady—my ideas need financial backing. How much would eyes in the back of our head cost? What about an extra hand? Oooh, massage chairs in the faculty lounge! An unlimited supply of our favorite pens! Okay, how about just swapping out water fountains for coffee fountains?

In case someone reading this has a money tree in their backyard, here are some other ideas that would help teachers do our job to the very best of our ability. Let me know if you're interested in sponsoring any of them. I'll get your name on a T-shirt or a plaque or something.

Increased Salary

Let's entertain the disgruntled taxpayers' notion that teachers are glorified babysitters. The average rate with a 1-child-to-1 babysitter ratio is $10 per hour. I'd imagine the rate increases as does the number of children (please hold while I do some math) . . . twenty-five children at $10 per hour is $250, times seven hours in a school day is $1,750, times the 180 days of the school year equals $315,000 a year! Teachers would be making serious bank! Okay, America, you are welcome to consider us babysitters; now pay us accordingly.

In-School Pharmacy

Here's something we can all agree on: Regardless of what we teach, our classrooms are giant cesspools. Students cough and sneeze on us, hand us pencils they've slobbered and gnawed on and their parents send them to school with fevers and the runs! If teachers are expected to endure 180 days of these conditions with limited sick time in the bank, at least give us a fighting chance. Every school should be equipped with its own stocked pharmacy where the necessities are readily available. Hook us up with an unlimited supply of Lysol wipes, tissues, hand sanitizer and alcohol. The rubbing kind or otherwise; let's not get caught up in minutiae. Once a year, I want a certified RN on standby, doling out flu shots like Oprah giving away Pontiac sedans: *You get a flu shot! You get a flu shot! Everyone gets a flu shot!*

Personal Assistant
Statistics show teachers will make up to 1,500 decisions every day. No wonder I can't remember my own name by three-thirty p.m. To conserve our brain power for more important tasks, might I suggest we delegate the menial yet necessary responsibilities to our personal assistants? There are too many days we're forced to choose between eating lunch sitting down, dropkicking the copy machine to churn out collated and stapled packets or using the restroom like a civilized human being. It'd be superfantastic to have a little help. Can we get a dedicated copy person? Someone to feed us? A wizard to configure (and reconfigure) the classroom seating arrangement most conducive to learning? I'm just spitballing here.

Policy-Making Power
For all the decisions educators are expected to make, I find it downright rude we're excluded when it comes to making the big ones. Why has no one invited me to the White House to discuss nationwide educational initiatives? Oh, that's right. Because it's easier to dangle a dollar sign like a carrot, essentially

forcing the change. I see you, Betsy! Teachers understand that it's time and involvement from all stakeholders that will make the biggest impact and hey, Washington, if you need ideas, let a girl know. Just so we're clear: *I am available for travel.*

Resident Therapists

Therapists should be on hand to address the physical and mental stressors of the job. Some should travel throughout the building, offering massages to weary teachers. Once our necks and shoulders and feet feel rejuvenated, we have the option of a happy ending. Instead of something salacious, the educator's happy ending is a new package of Flair pens.

As for our mental state, it goes without saying teaching isn't necessarily a low-stress job. What other profession consistently takes away preparation time yet increases its expectations for achievement or allows outsiders to influence best practices? Imagine the public outrage if the NFL were run like a public school: Players aren't given regular practice time but are still expected to bring home a Super Bowl ring, and if they don't deliver, the Monday morning quarterback with the biggest mouth jeopardizes their position on the team. There are literally talk shows dedicated to discussing athletic "travesties" like this, but ask the average Joe his opinion on the amount of time allotted for teachers' instructional prep, and he'll likely draw a blank.

Because teachers already feel unsupported and overwhelmed, guidance and career counseling should be available on-site. Therapists will implement a professional development series focused on self-care that includes such topics as the best time of the year to cash in a mental health day; how to cope with problematic students and asshole parents without drinking in the faculty lounge; Creative Cursing 101: how to swear at school without getting fired.

Dogs

Last, though certainly not least, I would like to please bring my dog to school with me. Research has proven time and time again being around animals, especially snuggly ones like my Charlie Bear, lowers blood pressure and stress levels. If that's not self-care, I don't know what is. I also know schools that bring dogs into the classroom so students can read to them without fear of judgment from their peers! *Can you even?!* Literacy and puppies go together better than chocolate and peanut butter, and that's the highest form of compliment coming from me. Basically, we need puppies all over the place. Thank you for coming to my TED Talk.

Since most of these asks are sadly unrealistic thanks to our country's lackluster investment in education, here are some practical tips to help you take care of yourself, fellow teacher.

My pals at We Are Teachers joined forces with teachers from Concordia University Portland's College of Education to come up with these achievable fixes, which are so easy we can all do them, such as leaving work *on time* twice a week. *Do it.* Here's another one: Don't bring your teacher bag home at least once a week. Maybe this day is Friday and you actually have a weekend—amazing! I asked my other teacher friends for their self-care ideas and this is what they said:

- Join an exercise challenge on social media or with friends (My kids' teachers do the Biggest Loser challenge every year—it's fun and healthy . . . says me, who doesn't participate.)
- Keep something yummy in your desk and don't share!
- Put something exciting on your calendar; studies show if we're looking forward to an event, we're happier.
- Spend time with colleagues outside of the school setting; the more you "gel," the stronger your team will be.
- Don't wait until you're physically ill to take a sick day—care for your mental health the way you would your body.
- Go for a walk on your lunch break.
- Learn the word no and use it whenever you're feeling overwhelmed. There's no shame in that.
- Do something that feeds your soul: Take an art class, blast music, go to church.

We can't control everything that happens in our school, or even in our day, but there are simple things we can do to improve our outlook. I'm not saying we have to Marie Kondo the crap out of our classrooms searching for the joy in our job, but . . . wait. That actually sounds amazing; someone call my personal assistant!

Leaving on time once a week or treating yourself to a gourmet coffee every Friday morning may seem insignificant at first, but you'll begin to really look forward to these things on a regular basis and that'll lift your spirits. Control the things you can. Whatever you do, I hope you find something that upgrades your day in a way that equals less stress and more happy, because we need you in our classrooms. You are important and valuable, dear educator, and we appreciate your service to our youth. Now, go! Sign up for a yoga class or throw axes (where legal and safe) and politely decline the invitation to proctor the SATs next Saturday because holy Common Core do you deserve a break!

Teacher Tip

Laugh so you don't cry. Or at least laugh after you cry.

The Time I Said the C-Word at a School Assembly (and Wasn't Fired!)

Before birthing my own offspring, I treated my students as though they were my own. I fussed over their accomplishments and embarrassed them with my happy crying and also pried into their personal lives because I was equal parts proud of and concerned about them. We challenged one another, both intellectually and emotionally, and it filled me up with a kind of professional and personal satisfaction I'd never quite felt before. I came to understand that teaching really is authentic preparation for parenthood: It's all giving kids their wings.

I took that obligation seriously, making a concerted effort to function as not only the students' teacher, but also their role model. It was important to me that I was viewed as an esteemed member of the faculty in and out of our classroom. Just as raising our own children is a heady responsibility, so too is maintaining a respectable reputation as an educator. As one of the younger teachers in our school, I was mindful of how everything from what I wore to what I said could impact my students, especially the females. I dedicated myself to careful choices that would serve as a positive example for them. Then, one day I said the word *cunt* at a school assembly.

WAIT! Don't leave!

Listen, don't tell my students, but I'm as vulgar as they come on a bad day. Even on a good day, I have been known to experiment with all the wonderful ways a gal can use the F-word. I don't blush at much, which I'm sure makes my parents proud, but *that* word, *the C-word*, is one of the few that makes me wince. Yet, I said it loud and proud into a microphone while standing onstage at a school-wide assembly.

Let's start at the beginning, shall we?

Our principals had organized an assembly to recognize our best students. The term *best* was meant to identify traditional academic successes, as well as the overlooked but applause-worthy achievements like behavior improvements and our football team's first female kicker. We wanted to shine a spotlight on the kids who, although deserving in their own right, rarely got to bask in its glow. The whole premise was enough to bring me to happy tears; I was so damn proud to be a teacher in *that* school to *those* students.

Watching as parents, school board members and other community stakeholders filed into our auditorium, my cup ranneth over. Moms and dads who had only previously visited the school to address their student's disciplinary issues were now smiling from ear to ear as we celebrated their children. There I was in my fancy suit, among colleagues who were also some of my favorite people in the whole world, thinking how very lucky I was to be a part of it all.

Finally, my turn came to introduce a group of students whose stellar work ethic was to be commended. Wrought with emotion, I took my place onstage, cleared my throat and then ruined everything with my poop mouth:

"Good afternoon!" I bellowed into the microphone. "I am so excited to recognize the amazing students seated behind me. Their cuntless . . . countless contributions to our school . . ."

Blah. Blah. Blah.

I could have announced the cure for cancer at that very moment and no one would have batted an eye since I, a pillar of the community, just blurted out the word *cuntless* in front of 500 people.

Time stopped. There was a ringing in my ears. I became hyperaware of a single bead of sweat that formed at my hairline and slowly trickled down my neck. I stood there, motionless, focusing on nothing but that trickle as it snaked the whole way down my back. A collective gasp from the students behind me jolted my attention back to reality. I heard one of them whisper, "Did she just say *that* word?"

She sure did.

I looked to the audience for support, or for someone to put me out of my misery, only to find my colleagues covering their mouths in shock. Eyes wide, deer in the headlights kind of thing. Acting like nothing out of the ordinary had happened, I said more words, desperately trying to salvage the rest of my speech. I couldn't make eye contact with anyone for fear of dropping dead right there on the stage. Instead, I stared at a spot on the wall while I spoke, pretending no one else was in the room. My efforts would have been successful had I not heard the muffled giggles. I allowed my eyes to wander just once and in time to see one of my favorite math teachers exiting the auditorium because he could no longer hold it together. Frantically, I scanned the other faces, hoping for solace, finding only scoffing.

I spent the remainder of the assembly staring at my shoes, wishing I could disappear. I will never forget the looks of agony/ embarrassment/amusement from the students *and* faculty as I completed the walk of shame back to my classroom. Some of them actually felt bad for me because seriously, who says *that word?!* Maybe a student slips and says it, but a teacher?! Many were quite happy to delight in my humiliation, recognizing it as the once-in-a-lifetime grand-scale mortification it was. Back at my desk, I opened an email from a colleague:

"Steph, we're doing happy hour after work. If you're hungry, I think the bar is running a special on cuntry-fried steak."

Messages like those bombarded my inbox for the rest of the day. I even got notes in my mailbox thanking me for *my* cuntless contributions to the assembly, which was lovely. Knowing I was shaken up by the whole experience, my principals sought me out to see if I was okay and offered support from our guidance cunteslor. . . .

I was horrified for having said that word, but mostly for taking the attention away from students who so deserved it and who rarely got it. I had ruined their moment and wondered if I'd ruined my reputation in the process. I wrestled with whether an apology was the right thing to do. Although revisiting the snafu felt wildly inappropriate, I recognized the teachable moment in allowing myself to be vulnerable in front of the kids. I was scared and embarrassed, but the elephant in the room was towering over us, and I knew I had to take care of it.

When I apologized, I expected the students to giggle or hit me with looks of disgust, but they extended such grace. No laughing, no judging and no one seemed to think any less of me. The positive role model reputation I'd worked hard to build was thankfully still intact. "My kids" accepted my apology and we moved on. It was that simple.

Therein lies the beauty of teenagers: They're always messing up, so they're familiar with being under the microscope of criticism and judgment. I thought one, albeit gigantic, mistake would change their perception of me, but they gave me what they wanted in return: understanding and forgiveness.

As for the administrators and community members who witnessed my display of inadvertent vulgarity, fortunately, we were a small district, one with a good sense of humor, and I retained my job despite my mistake. But my pride? That's long gone.

Teacher Tip

Embrace Monday, and all the challeneges it presents.

Teamwork, Honest Dialogue and Pizza: A Recipe for Improving Your School

My first in-service day as a new hire at Hill High School was not a typical one. Instead of procedural stuffs, the other newbies and I piled into a district van driven by our head principal and toured the dilapidated remnants of a once bustling small town. These neighborhoods, plagued with condemned buildings and vacant houses, were home to our incoming students. Our principal was adamant we witness how and where many of our students lived, but even as she made frequent stops to say hello to smiling groups of kids, I couldn't help feeling uneasy.

Kids barely old enough to tie their own shoes were hanging out on street corners, near homemade signs and crosses marking the spot of murder victims. Storefronts were boarded up and the ones that remained open had bars in their windows and signs promising the clerks kept only $100 in the register at all times. I guess if the iron bars weren't deterrent enough, the minimal cash would make a lazy thief think twice?

More than half our students were economically disadvantaged, and as research and experience have consistently shown, poverty and formal education aren't exactly friends. This eye-opening neighborhood tour aimed to show us what we'd be up against once the kids entered our classrooms. Many of them came to school for nothing more than a hot meal and to socialize. My English class wasn't their priority because their struggle to meet basic needs overshadowed any educational effort. As far as they were concerned, learning wasn't all that important, and there was no one at home telling them any differently. I was fortunate to already have a good relationship with the handful of students I'd met teaching in summer school, but that didn't make me immune to the problems at Hill High that came between students and their education.

Fights broke out pretty regularly, with what started in the neighborhoods spilling over into our hallways. I eventually learned it was safe to jump in the middle of boys because even though they didn't think twice about wailing on one another, they never threw a punch if it meant putting a female teacher in harm's way. Girls, on the other hand, were a different story. Girls were savage. I'd be bald and bloody if I dared to break up a girl fight, so I usually let my larger-than-five-foot-one male colleagues handle those ones.

In addition to trying to keep the peace, colleagues and I

recognized our curriculum and special education program needed a major facelift if we hoped to reach these students. While we did have rays of sunshine poke through the academic clouds every now and again, test scores and graduation rates spoke mostly of the storm. We knew we had to do something, and the one-size-fits-all government-mandated initiatives weren't going to cut it. So instead, we took a chance on each other.

We started by choosing unusual allies and promising them pizza. Our head and assistant principals handpicked students with clear—though unconventional—leadership skills in hopes they would become our liaisons. One such leader was a notorious hall wanderer with failing grades who was known for participating in questionable after-school activities. Ahem. But we saw his potential and made the most of it. He and others showed up to our clandestine meetings because they heard there would be food; they stayed because we stressed their important role in the school, emphasizing the ways they were valuable to our overall success, which I believe was a first for those kids.

We talked. A lot. We talked about race and learning, poverty and learning, gender and learning, reputation and learning. One boy admitted he wanted to do better in school but wouldn't be caught dead carrying books home, so we gave him a complete set of textbooks to keep at his place. We explained what we saw in each of them that could positively affect change in our current school climate, and they seemed surprised we'd noticed. Highlighting each of their attributes, we spitballed different ways they could benefit our school.

A girl who was adept at diffusing stressful situations with humor, laughing off academic frustrations that would otherwise escalate, could help ease other struggling students' tension and confusion, making learning a better experience for everyone.

A varsity wrestler's tenacity and get-after-it attitude on the mat could carry over into math.

Another athlete who regularly stepped off the football field and onto the stage for the spring musical could help continue smashing stereotypes in the classroom. If he started contributing to class discussions, others would take notice and do the same.

Considered a natural leader, a junior girl's willingness to calm the hell down during lunch effectively persuaded others to follow suit, and she helped change the cafeteria from a battleground to . . . well, a cafeteria.

Once our students realized we truly believed in them and saw potential in their wonderful qualities, they began acting with a sense of purpose. We were thrilled with the extent to which the students bought in and capitalized on the momentum with a new school-wide initiative: Hill PRIDE, which stood for "Personal Responsibility in Daily Efforts." PRIDE adorned every classroom wall and was at the core of all we did, proving that working together toward the same goals, celebrating one another's successes and investing in one another was worthwhile for morale and academics. After a few more meetings, and a lot of praise and pizza, our school began to see real change.

After-school tutoring attendance increased once the "cool" kids began going. Fighting and off-task behavior decreased now that the instigators were on our team and in class. I crap you not: One of our juniors wrote and performed a rap song about the importance of the PSSAs (Pennsylvania's standardized tests at the time). Our administrators' vision, that those students would become our allies, came to fruition and lifted up the entire school.

The foundation was laid; now it was time for us to build.

Teachers needed time to collaborate and communicate, but the in-service days and faculty meetings just weren't enough. Our principals heard us and modified the school's entire schedule to accommodate collaborative time every Monday morning. What a huge difference that made! Each department was hard at work updating the curriculum, designing formative assessments and analyzing the data that then informed our instruction. All high school teachers began implementing the same organizational writing strategy, 4-Square, and after a brief time, we saw improvement in student writing across the board. Our department chair (who is surely a saint) gifted us binders of our new curriculum, equipped with the big ideas and essential questions (aligned with state performance standards—swoon!) that served as a guide for every English classroom. The only thing more beautiful than our curriculum binders were the ones she created for our students: Kids received PSSA binders, complete with glossaries, equation sheets and the fabulous 4-Square. Told ya she's a saint!

To more accurately track the improvements, our principals asked for the big D. Calm down, I'm talking about data. Teachers in each subject area created and administered the same assessments—we named them "APS," or assessments of performance standards—then used the results to identify student learning strengths and weaknesses. APS provided in-depth data that allowed us to pinpoint such things as which standards most often tripped up students, which groups of students needed remediation, which students were rocking it and could help with said remediation and how a bit of self-reflection could improve our instruction. It was daunting because the data meant more work for us, but anything worth doing is hard. And we did the hard stuff, together. That Monday morning time was a unicorn. Our schoolwide collaboration and consistency were turning out results. With our positive relationships and motivation fueling our students' academic efforts, they were more open to learning, and it showed in their achievement. We were headed in the right direction but still needed to find better ways to serve our large special education population.

As with most things in education, one step forward often results in the need to take a few backward first. As someone with a limited special ed background, I was finding it increasingly difficult to reach every kid on his/her level during one class period. To help remedy this issue, our principals dedicated professional development days to collaborative methods, specifically the coteaching model. I was one of the lucky ducks to pair up with an incredible special education teacher who eventually became my right-hand (wo)man. We used our Monday morning time to acclimate her to the material, since so much of it was brand-new to her, and she helped shape my instructional methods to be more special ed–friendly. During class, she dove in headfirst, taking diligent notes alongside the students while I led class discussions using her pointers. She even completed the same homework assignments! Students giggled as she scrawled reading reminders in her notebook and raised her hand to ask questions, but seeing her in student mode modeled effective active learning and study skills for the others. She committed 110 percent to her new role, and before long, she and I were expertly tag-teaming our English classroom. We were able to implement different strategies during the same class period—small group instruction, large group instruction, enrichment, intervention—and it was all possible with collaboration.

Inspired by our high school's success, the entire district adopted 4-Square, and PSSA scores went through the roof after that. Student writing scores were in the 90th percentile that year with graduation rates following in hot pursuit. My colleagues and I dedicated more time, energy and paychecks to those students than we ever admitted to the negative Nellies who kept telling us "that's not part of your job!" Thankfully, their words fell on deaf ears; we knew our school, our kids, our time together was special. We took a chance and it paid off. We did it our way and defied the odds. Never again have I witnessed or been a part of something quite like it. We did what the cynics said we couldn't. We succeeded where the naysayers said we wouldn't. We flourished where statistics said we shouldn't.

We did it.

We did the hell out of it.

Together.

Teacher Truth

Things teachers lose sleep over: our students, testing, our students, the beginning of the school year, our students.

part III
New Year, Who Dis?

Teacher Tip

**Don't view change as a challenge.
Look at it as an opportunity.**

Pumping in the Teachers' Lounge

Hello, my name is Stephanie, and I was four months pregnant the first time I was shamed for wanting a career *and* a family.

The year 2009 was a big one for me: I was at a new school, set to deliver both a new Advanced Placement curriculum and my first baby. While my husband and I had been talking about growing our family, my English department had been trying to increase our AP offerings. Ever the multitasker, I tackled these giant tasks simultaneously.

It was early February when I announced my pregnancy at school. I would've waited longer, but I had already started showing, and I felt compelled to explain why my ankles had become one with my calves. Also, the noise my female coworkers made upon hearing my news reverberated through the school and I had no choice but to fess up. Those women enveloped me in hugs, squealing at decibels only dogs can hear. We jumped up and down, wrapped in one another's arms, because, babiesssss!!! Male colleagues wished me well from a respectful distance, perhaps concerned my condition was contagious. Some students applauded, as though having unprotected sex was quite the accomplishment. I felt my cheeks flush when a sophomore boy was like, "Great job, Mrs. J!"

Ummmm . . . thank you?

Among all the warm and happy sentiments, my principal's reaction is what has stuck with me all this time. No hug, no congratulations, just, "You're going to finish that AP curriculum, right?"

He took the wind right outta my pregnant sails. I shouldn't have been as surprised or as hurt as I was; those who came before me had cautioned: having kids can jeopardize things for teachers, especially us moms. Sure, dads face their own version of professional ostracism to a certain extent, but their experiences seem to be few and far between as compared to moms'.

It's no secret most working women struggle to find a balance between their professional and personal lives, and teachers are no different. Coworkers have shared stories of how their colleagues and administrators became agitated when motherhood necessitated they use (contractually provided, theirs-for-the-taking, completely legitimate) sick days to care for their children. Many of these same women had duties and courses reassigned, perceived as unreliable once they became mothers. Breastfeeding mamas encountered next-level struggles when needing to pump at work; an open faculty lounge or classroom certainly didn't provide privacy, even with a closed door, and who wants to sit on a dirty toilet while expressing milk for their baby?

When familial priorities took precedence and these teacher-moms could no longer meet unwritten expectations like attending after-school school events, they were labeled as disinterested or worse, a burden. The "you owe me" mentality seemingly only affected moms. Case in point: A female colleague recalled a time she needed coverage at the end of the day to take her child to a doctor's appointment; it was held over her head until she "repaid the favor." In contrast, coaches leaving for games or teachers attending personal appointments were given no-strings-attached, no-questions-asked coverage. Double-standard much?

So there I was, expecting for the first time, and already my professional commitment was being called into question: "You're going to finish that AP curriculum, right?"

It has been more than a decade, and I'm still mad at myself for not throwing my principal some expert-level shade. Instead, I did what a "good" employee does and assured him I would have the curriculum on the college board's desk before the baby came. I had a late July due date and stupid amounts of naivety that newborns were naturally accommodating.

Bless my heart.

On a balmy July evening, I tempted the birthing gods by accompanying family to Pittsburgh for my brother's 25th birthday celebration at Hofbräuhaus. Nothing screams *classy* like a very pregnant woman at a German brewery shouting *"Shotski! Shotski!"* as inebriated strangers chug *hefeweizen*.

I went into labor later that night and still blame those hard, wooden benches.

After three hours of unsuccessful pushing, I was wheeled into the OR for an emergency caesarian section. The only reason I mention this in a book about education is because I need you to understand something very important: I lost my damn mind that night. Doctors sawed me in half, extracted a tiny human, and when they put me back together, my heart had been permanently removed from my chest cavity and placed inconveniently and precariously on my sleeve. Any semblance of logic and reason I had previously possessed disappeared along with my waistline.

Never having experienced such terrifying rapture in all my life, I was overcome with love . . . and a lot of pain. I sat in my ice-packed undies, incision throbbing, staring at my perfect baby boy. *I seriously made that.*

A month later, my colleagues were reporting for duty as the new school year loomed. A small part of me missed it, but a bigger part was being tortured by what I now refer to as an Internal Maternal Freak-Out: I was suddenly smitten with the desire to never ever leave my house again. Ever.

Please recall what I said about my diminished capacity for logic and reason.

After discussing our financial situation, my husband and I determined we could only make do without my paycheck until the new year. Shout-out to America's horrific maternity/ paternity leave.

So began my short stint as a stay-at-home mom. Because

my son was the first grandchild, family paid us daily visits, enthralled with every baby coo and sneeze. I was showered with gifts, meals, offers to fold laundry so I could nap. I had more help and support than the average mother and for that, I am eternally grateful. My body was healing; my brain was functioning. I began recognizing myself in the mirror again. The first months of my son's life were a love fest, and we relished every second of it.

But then I got bored.

At first, I was afraid to admit it, and braced for the backlash any time I confessed what felt like a cardinal sin: I couldn't ignore the growing urge for intelligent conversation and adult interaction.

I missed challenging my students.

I missed collaborating with my colleagues.

I did not miss having to wear real pants.

It's not that I didn't enjoy motherhood (though tedious at times), but I was suddenly adamant that I needed "more." Complicating these feelings was the fact that I was also adamant about not leaving my child. I felt like someone was forcing me to choose between the two loves of my life. My degree was nagging me, elbowing me in the ribs like, "Hey, remember how you busted your butt for me? Remember how hard it was to get a dang job and now you want to walk away? You can't just forget about all our professional goals!"

Just when I thought I'd convinced myself to head back to the classroom, Mommy Guilt reared her ugly head and shook a maternal finger in my face: "Nuh-uh, lady. Your child needs you. What kind of a mother chooses other kids over her own?" My professional and personal lives continued to duke it out until one night I broke down sobbing while hooked up to my hands-free breast pump. My husband walked in the room just in time to witness the hot mess that was his wife: a half-naked woman sobbing into a burp cloth while a whirring machine milked her like a dairy cow.

"I can't leave the baby!"

"I can't *not* teach!"

"There is no middle ground. *Why is there no middle ground?*"

My sweet husband, thoroughly confused and perhaps a little afraid, kissed the top of my head and quickly retreated. Poor guy just didn't get it. Recalling my principal's crappy congratulations, I considered where his priorities would lie if I returned. He certainly didn't get it. All the online forums full of new, anticareer mothers professing a 1,000 percent commitment to their babies clearly didn't get it, either. Where were the other women who wanted the best of both worlds? And why did I feel so freaking alone in my desire to be both Mommy and Mrs. J.? Sufficiently frustrated and unable to articulate exactly what I was feeling, I sought out the one source of comfort that has never let me down: Google.

At two a.m., I searched, "Can I teach from home?" and was shocked to learn I could! I clicked on the first school in the results and fired off an email with my résumé attached.

It seemed like a long shot, but I woke the next morning feeling optimistic anyway. I was empowered by simply having a choice. Taking a step toward teaching from home made me feel like a badass, like I was reclaiming a part of myself that had been dormant since giving birth. Society has a whole bunch of stupid rules for working women, especially working mothers, and as one who has never taken kindly to being told what to do, I was proud of myself for forging a new path. I was ready to be the exception to the rules, especially since it meant giving my child what he needed—me—and giving myself what I needed—my teaching career. Of course, I encountered the pearl-clutching backlash of those who firmly believed I was being a selfish mother; a family member actually called me the F-word like it was a bad thing:

Feminist.

If a feminist is someone who goes after what she needs to be the best version of herself, then color me #sorrynotsorry because now that I knew there was a way to remain in the world of education while raising my baby, I was ready for the next step.

Just had to wait for my breasts to stop leaking. After that, I was so ready.

Teacher Truth

Teaching won't make you tons of money, but it sure will make you rich.

Good-Bye Classroom, Hello Computer

The day I walked into the beautiful blank slate that was my very first classroom, the heavens opened and the angels sang. It was either that or the humming from the fluorescent lighting. I spent years in that same room, pouring blood, sweat and tears into my craft. It was such a worthwhile job, fulfilling me and giving me purpose like nothing in life ever had. Those students, that classroom, were my passion.

Then, I had my own kids.

You wanna talk passion? I was stupid with it. When my son was a few weeks old, a woman stopped us in the grocery store to compliment his ocean-blue eyes and ask his name; I smiled proudly and responded, "Eli." My son's name is Brady. So, maybe passion isn't the correct term to describe my early experiences with motherhood, but let's just say whatever I was feeling was certainly all-encompassing. Maybe I didn't know his name, but I did know I'd break someone's kneecaps for him.

Although my brief stretch as a stay-at-home-mom proved I wasn't ready to cut all ties with my career, it gave me precious time to reevaluate my professional goals. A two-a.m. email inquiring about the possibility of teaching cyberschool resulted in my first-ever conference call, which, I learned, was the virtual equivalent of an interview. During the call with a lovely woman named Janice, my son Brady—not Eli—started fussing in the background. I apologized for the interruption, and Janice quickly but kindly reprimanded me: "Don't ever apologize for doing your job. The women before us have apologized enough."

Whoa. Tears sprung up in my eyes, and I bit down on the inside of my cheek to keep my voice from quivering. Janice hadn't a clue how powerful her words were; they summed up everything I'd be feeling about the push and pull of balancing motherhood and teaching.

After a third call with Janice, aka the final-round interview, she submitted my name for hire. She then did me another, perhaps more significant, solid and told me not to accept the first offer. I understood the cyber position wouldn't be a salaried one in the beginning, but I hadn't realized I would have the power to negotiate the pay rate. I'd never countered any offer before, not at the movie theater where I'd worked in high school nor at the bakery where I'd worked hungover in college, and certainly not at my current brick-and-mortar teaching gig. Janice could have easily withheld the negotiation tip, making her higher-up happy by saving the company money. Instead she gave me a seat at the table. Her gesture said, "You have control and your input matters." In doing so, she established a foundation of trust and collaboration, making me feel valuable and respected as a woman *and* an educator, which wasn't exactly the vibe my former principal had been giving me.

I was ready to sign on the dotted line. Hell, I was ready to give Janice a lap dance. But before I could do anything, I wanted to be certain the move to cyberschool was the right one for our family, so my husband and I did the adult thing and made a list of pros and cons:

Pros of teaching cyberschool:
- I'd be home with my son
- We could maintain two incomes, sort of

- We'd save money on:
  - Childcare
  - My school clothes
  - Classroom supplies
  - Wear-and-tear on the car
  - Those lattes I treated myself to every morning before work . . .

Cons of teaching cyberschool:
- Huge pay cut
- Less money meant things like my master's work would be put on hold

- Uncertainty: Would I like virtual education? Did it have staying power?
- Suspicious of this newfangled "direct deposit" stuff: Was it a hoax? Would I really be paid?

I tend to worry less about finances and more about happiness, and my husband is the opposite. When it comes to money, I'm basically a hippie in a field of daisies lighting dollar bills and my bra on fire. My husband is a three-piece suit with a briefcase. That's why I was pleasantly surprised to find we agreed that this leap could work for our family. I made it clear teaching from home didn't mean he'd find me in heels and an apron, and he made me promise to address my Amazon Prime addiction. I accepted the job and submitted my letter of resignation to my brick-and-mortar school.

It has been more than a decade since I traded in my classroom for a computer, and I'm happy to report direct deposit turned out to be a thing. I'm now a mother of three; that blue-eyed baby boy has two sisters. Thanks to teaching remotely, I don't have to take a day off when one of my kiddos is sick; plus the more flexible schedule allows me to do things like volunteer at their schools and get them on and off the bus every day. I'd initially been skeptical of virtual education's "staying power," but I got my foot in the door just as it started picking up momentum. For the first time in my life, I was on the cutting edge of something. I don't want to brag, but some consider my job trendy. *sips chamomile tea and adjusts drawstring sweatpants*

Buuuuuuuut . . . teaching from home isn't perfect.

Many virtual teaching positions are actually affiliated with a company, not a school. So, that turns education into a business, which adds unnecessary red tape to the job. For instance, I can't add outside content to my classes, even if I find a kickass resource my students would love. Copyright laws and company policy interfere with something as simple as beefing up my curriculum. Additionally, that curriculum is usually set, giving teachers little input. Some find this refreshing, but control freaks like me find it frustrating.

Teaching remotely, while flexible, is still a job, and there are real people relying on me. I think too many educators (and students) enter the world of virtual education with expectations that it'll be easy and not require much effort. *Lies.* It's different, but it's still demanding. You're doing it from home, but that only adds another layer of difficulty, in my opinion. The schedule is more forgiving, but there are still deadlines, and those deadlines are kinda hard to meet if you have a baby on your boob or a sick kid home from school vying for your time.

Speaking of kids, I really do miss interacting with students face-to-face. I want to see their new haircuts and ridiculous fashion trends and high-five them as they walk into class. In my current position, it's just not possible. For the last few years of my virtual teaching job, my students have lived in different states, so meeting them in person is basically a no-go. That said, I find ways to make those important connections and sincerely believe I still have an impact on their education, especially those who are working toward their diploma.

I just wish I could see them in their cap and gown, walking across the stage. I'm social by nature, and never anticipated how emotionally draining and isolating it could be to stay cooped up in the house so much. After some trial and error (read: many meltdowns by yours truly), my husband began encouraging me to get out more often. When he's like, "Call your friends and leave the house immediately," I know it's time to wash my hair and get my socializing on. Whaddya know, it helps! I've used my experiences to bridge the social gap between me and my students, who have similar feelings.

Oh, and let me caution you of something else I hadn't originally considered: Working remotely means you're sitting for the majority of the day, whereas in the traditional classroom, we're on our feet constantly. At first, this was a welcomed change of pace, especially with three little ones underfoot. Sitting down felt like a vacation! But ten years and a couple larger pant sizes later, there are now days I have to remind myself to stand up! It's easy to get locked in and lose hours staring at a screen, especially when your side hustle is writing. I've really had to dedicate myself to exercise, which I hate with every fiber of my being. But much like putting on a bra and leaving the house, working out energizes me. And keeps me healthier blahblahblah.

Having my entire life exist in the same space, at the same time used to make it difficult to separate what I should be doing vs. what I wanted to be doing. In the beginning, I never logged off. Literally. I would be checking email while tucking my kids in at night or taking calls at the playground. I had to train myself to create a healthy balance, which proved necessary when I found myself waking in the middle of the night to check just one more essay. I learned the hard way to set limits for myself, otherwise I risked being plugged in all day, every day and missing out on the things that enticed me to teach from home in the first place. Slowly, a routine started to emerge, and that's what saved my sanity. We created a dedicated work space for all my teaching stuff in a home office, and I stopped using the couch as a desk. Those physical boundaries were visible reminders of when I should be working and when I shouldn't be. I also started doing this crazy thing where I'd take a lunch break and walk away from my computer for 30 minutes. *Amazing.* When my kids napped, I got more done in those two hours than in the rest of my day. When it was quitting time, I quit. I stopped checking emails at night, and when I felt everything building up, I gave my husband a friendly heads-up *before* I snapped. I'm a good wife like that.

I've also gotten better at minimizing the multitasking, which is the opposite of what corporate America wants us to do. Listen, I refuse to believe I'm doing *better* just because I'm doing *more*. We're so work-obsessed and product-driven that we feel inferior if we're not willingly overwhelming ourselves with a multitude of tasks, juggling a dozen things at a time just because we can. So much of success is managing our time and properly prioritizing tasks. Having the word *no* in our vocabulary helps, too. When people hear I teach online, they assume I'm available for all the things since they confuse working from home with napping all day. . . .

PTA mom: Since you work from home, can you volunteer at the school every day?

Me: No.

Friend: Since you work from home, can you babysit my two-year-old a few times a week?

Me: No.

Husband: Since you're working from home, can we get rid of the cleaning service?

Me: Hell-to-the-no.

Today, I'm a full-time, salaried virtual educator. A simple Google search, tons of determination and a pinch of crying made my vision a reality. I know it's not everyone's cup of tea, and that's okay. That's the beauty of options. I've never missed a day with my children, who are now all in school, and there's no gap on my teaching résumé. I don't know where the future will take my career, but I have every intention of remaining open to all possibilities. Hashtag blessed.

Virtual Versions of Annoying Colleagues

Names have been changed to protect the identity of the irritating.

At the beginning of my career in virtual education, I longed for familiarity. I missed parts of the job that I'd inadvertently taken for granted while working in the traditional school setting: seeing peoples' faces when we talked, yukking it up in the faculty lounge, taking pride in my appearance. On a day I was especially lamenting the things that were no longer, a big ol' piece of familiar plopped into my inbox.

Upon opening the email, I came face-to-face with fellow teacher Ann's message blasting our company's new initiative. Ann was either oblivious of or simply IDGAF about the fact that she included our direct supervisor on her gripe. I sat back at my desk and waited for the magic to unfold.

Ping!

Karen responds almost immediately in resounding agreement with her girl Ann.

Ping!

Carl, who is retired from the public school system and only in virtual education as a "hobby," shares his disdain of the additional workload.

Ping!

Tom sends a "thumbs-down" emoji, the professional equivalent of the middle finger.

Ping! Ping! Ping!

At our next staff meeting, we're forced to endure a 25-minute presentation about tone in writing. We are encouraged to put our best virtual foot forward in emails and learn to temper our emotions before pressing send. As the monotone speaker mercilessly blathers on about a topic we've already covered eleventy billion times, it hits me: The annoying colleagues I fondly remember from my former school still exist! Although there are special nuances to these new digital versions, my coworkers in the virtual space are all too familiar. . . .

Brown-Nose Barb: Look, I appreciate Barb. She's always first to volunteer, she's efficient and productive, and if you're lucky enough to be on her team, you look good by association. But Barb is so far up the boss's arse that she cannot be trusted with the fun stuff. Play nice but withhold all inappropriate jokes and silly complaints. You have been warned.

Busier-Than-You Brian: In a traditional school setting, you'd recognize Brian as always rushing around, scarfing down lunch at his desk and loudly announcing how busy he is. In a remote setting, Brian's exasperated sigh precedes his every word, and he always manages to mention how many essays he has to grade or how his class sizes are through the roof. Brian is no busier than the rest of us and is likely just pretending to be swamped so no one asks more of him. Wait a minute. Brian is a genius.

Conflict Carla: Doesn't matter what the topic is, Conflict Carla has beef with it. She will go toe-to-toe with you, with the boss, with the students, with any policy. Conflict Carla must have some hidden talent the rest of us don't know about because there's no other explanation for how she remains employed.

Friday Frank: Frank's a real douchebag who insists on emailing everyone an hour before quitting time on Friday. The rest of us are mentally checked out and he wants to go over reports, discuss a game plan for next week or call a "real quick meeting to get all our ducks in a row." Frank needs a hobby.

Negative Nancy: Since you're not in the same room with Negative Nancy, it's impossible to witness her signature eye rolls during conversation. To remedy this, Nance peppers her emails with ominous ellipses and straight up dissention:

I'm very disappointed by what we're told is "best practice." I imagine there would be legal ramifications, but I guess we don't have a teacher's union, so . . .

Passive-Aggressive Paul: If a colleague has ever prefaced an answer to your question with, "as I previously stated" or "please refer to my original message for more information," you've been Paul-verized. Admittedly, I am passive-aggressive Paul, but at least I know how to show restraint, courtesy of all those helpful staff meetings. . . .

Positive Patty: While she's not surly and Eeyore-ish like some of her colleagues, Patty's "look on the bright side" perspective kinda makes you want to punch kittens. Like, I'm having a bad day, okay, Patty? Can you reel it in just a bit, Patty? It doesn't sound like I'm smiling because *I'm not, Patty.*

Reply-All Robert: Robert's favorite thing in life is hitting the Reply All option when responding to a mass email. Bad form, Robert. No one except your supervisor cares that you have follow-up questions regarding last week's training or that you are so on board with the school's new attendance policy. *Get out of my inbox, Robert.*

Shorthand Shannon: SMH[1], I cannot even with this one. Srsly[2]. UR[3] sending a professional msg[4]; is the recipient not worth full words? FFS[5]. Do better, Shannon. TY[6].

---

[1] Shaking My Head
[2] Seriously
[3] You Are
[4] message
[5] For Fuck's Sake
[6] Thank You

Team-Player Trevor: "Let me know if you need anything!" is Trevor's signature move. He actually means it, too, which is weird because most people just say it because it's more polite than, "We're done here, bye." Anyway, if you need someone to pull those reports or dissect any of that data, Trevor is your man. Tip: Make Trevor your friend.

One-Up Wanda: Wanda never misses a chance to refer to the prestigious university she attended or work her extravagant weekend plans into the conversation. Whatever you're doing at work, Wanda has been there and done that *better*. Don't feel inferior, though; feel bad for Wanda, as she's probably compensating for feelings of inadequacy that stem from childhood and have since infiltrated her professional life and now she struggles with self-esteem issues. I'm just guessing.

There are many upsides to dealing with the virtual versions of annoying colleagues, namely they can't see when you roll your eyes or flip them off. Not that I ever do those things . . .

Teacher Tip

Expect the best and plan for the worst. But learn to roll with the punches no matter what.

Seventeen-Inch Plate

I come from a baseball family. One of my mom's cousins played in the pros, another coached at a Division I university and another dated former All-Star second baseman and coach Mickey Morandini. While I was growing up, summers revolved around my and my brother's softball and baseball schedules; I remember having to cut our beach vacations short so we'd be home in time for our All-Star games. I turned out to be a half-decent softball player, but my brother, Mike, was the true standout. It's because of Mike's baseball career that I scored me a husband.

While I was away at college studying to be a teacher, Zach was already teaching and coaching at my brother's high school. It seemed like every time I called home, the conversation ended with my mom gushing about Mike's baseball coach: "He's soooo handsome!" I made a point to find out for myself, and the second I laid eyes on Zach, I made every effort to get to more of my brother's games.

Sixteen years and three kids later, Zach and I still make a good team, and I continue overusing baseball metaphors to describe our relationship. As teachers, we both appreciate how a good baseball-themed cliché effortlessly lends itself to education, and it was Zach who first introduced me to the story of the seventeen-inch plate. Although the story's premise revolves around the game of baseball, it's hard to ignore the correlation to today's classrooms.

In 1996, 78-year-old collegiate hall of fame baseball coach John Scolinos was the featured speaker at a national baseball coaches' convention. When he took the stage with a regulation-sized home plate tied around his neck, Scolinos's captive audience of 4,000 coaches automatically assumed his age had caught up to him. Exacerbating their concerns, Scolinos kept repeating the same question: "How wide is home plate?"

He asked the Little League coaches; they replied, "Seventeen inches."

He asked the college coaches; they answered, "Seventeen inches."

When the question finally reached the major league coaches, everyone was yelling, "Seventeen inches!"

Amid the snickering, Scolinos then asked what coaches should do if a pitcher couldn't hit his targets over the seventeen inches: "Do we make it eighteen inches or nineteen inches . . . do we make it twenty inches so [the pitcher has] a better chance of hitting it?" Like a steam engine gaining speed, Scolinos continued: "What do we do when our best player shows up late to practice? When our team rules forbid facial hair and a guy shows up unshaven? What if he gets caught drinking? Do we hold him accountable? Or do we change the rules to fit him? Do we widen home plate?"

Silence.

Scolinos then took out a marker and drew a school on the previously stark white surface dangling from his neck, explaining we've been guilty of widening the plate in our schools: "The quality of our education is going downhill fast and teachers have been stripped of the tools they need to be successful, and to educate and discipline our young people. We are allowing others to widen home plate! Where is that getting us?"

Now you're nodding along.

We've all widened the proverbial plate for our students a time or two; that's not what Coach Scolinos was talking about. When "widening" becomes the norm, the expectation, and educators become complacent pawns in the game, students and schools suffer the innate consequences. How many of you have been told to "find a creative way to pass" a failing student? Who among us hasn't felt pressure from a principal, guidance counselor, coach, parent or even ourselves to "bump up" a kid's grade? We're constantly asked to make concessions for academic achievement, effectively training students to expect the standards will change to meet them and not the other way around.

I worked at a high school where all students had to complete a senior project as a graduation requirement. We teachers served as their academic mentors, providing feedback and guidance as needed. Full days were set aside for the students to present their projects to a board of teachers and administrators and, as was expected, some didn't show. They offered lame excuses and tired explanations in place of the finished product. We recognized this as stage fright and gave them a second chance, even allowing these students to handpick the board that would assess their projects, thinking that would give them enough confidence to follow through. It was enough for some, but others remained hyperanxious about the presentations, and slowly but surely, I found we were cutting corners in a way that compromised the expectations of the project. When word got out that there were students who didn't have to fulfill the requirements in the same way, we had some pretty pissed-off people on our hands. Parents, students, other teachers, you name it. We thought we were helping by being understanding, but in actuality, our accommodations were a version of widening the plate.

Maybe you've not been in the same situation as my senior project fiasco, but I'm willing to bet some of these look familiar:

The football team's quarterback hasn't turned in his research paper, turning his overall grade into a failing one. Does his English teacher wait to add the zero to the gradebook so he's eligible on Friday night or does she make him turn in the work and earn his spot in the game?

One of the school's most gifted musicians hasn't been coming to school and when she is there, she sleeps in class. When the band director receives an invitation for the student to play with the city's professional symphony, should he ignore her apathetic attitude and terrible attendance and allow her to go, or let real-life consequences teach her a lesson?

The wrestling playoffs are on Saturday and the team's lightweight champ is caught with marijuana on Thursday. As per school policy, the drugs should be immediately turned over to the police and the wrestler suspended from school for five days. Do administrators wait to address the infraction to benefit the wrestling team or follow the district's protocol?

In early May, a senior student's behavior becomes increasingly disruptive. Does the school administration send her home for the remainder of the year, freezing her grades to ensure she graduates (yes, this actually happens), or do they hold her to the same standards as all the other seniors?

One of your AP students travels a lot throughout the school year. As a result, his grades have started to slip, and his parents ask you to exempt some of the work. Do you modify his workload or cite his travel as a privilege and the class as his responsibility?

The line between an understanding, empathetic educator and one who constantly widens the plate isn't as fine as some may think. If you make a habit out of lowering your standards to accommodate students, instead of helping students rise up and meet your standards, you are widening the plate. As with anything in life, what's easier can be tempting because it requires us to *give* less: less time, less energy, less effort.

If you're satisfied with *getting* less as a result, by all means widen that plate. If, however, you hold yourself to a higher standard when [fill-in-the-blank]—parenting, coaching, teaching, singing, creating—you understand the benefits of giving more. And if anyone deserves more, a full seventeen inches, it's the young minds that will one day lead our country.

"The TV Hacked My Laptop" and More Ridiculous 21st-Century Student Excuses

All teachers have their own book-worthy tales of the crazy lengths their students have gone to avoid doing their work or to justify their inappropriate behavior. As a cyber-school teacher, I am not immune to these outlandish student excuses. In fact, virtual learning has introduced new ways for students and their parents to pass the (digital) buck while effectively kicking common courtesy to the curb. All that to say: Technology makes it way too easy for people to be lazy and rude! The only difference between the traditional excuses and the virtual ones is the role technological bravado and confusion play in them.

Technical glitches are inevitable. Things like scheduled maintenance and temporary crashes can interfere with students' access to their classes. Sometimes, though, the problem is user-error, which is a nice way of saying, *"You're the problem, Karen!"* With a decade of cyberschool under my belt, I've grown used to the imperfect nature of technology and have come to expect these things. Well, some of these things. . . .

My Smart TV Made Me Do It

Me, calling home: Your daughter hasn't submitted work in a few days. Is everything okay?

Mom: Actually, we're having problems with our television. My daughter said our smart TV hacked her laptop and that's why she can't work.

Me: Ma'am, it is not possible for your smart TV to hack your daughter's computer. I can see activity in her account that proves she is able to log in; she's simply not doing the work. I think she's pulling the wool over your eyes.

Mom: She wouldn't do that. I'm going to call our Internet provider and figure this out.

I wasted hours of my life that I'll never get back waiting for the Internet provider to tell Mom the same thing: Her daughter was playing her. It made me sad to think a child would exploit her own mother's ignorance just to avoid doing schoolwork. I banged my head on my desk in a show of solidarity for mothers everywhere.

Plug-in Problems

Student: I'm calling to let you know I won't be able to work today.

Me: Oh, no! Why not?

Student: I'm having trouble plugging in.

Me: Do you mean a plug-in isn't compatible with your computer?

Student: No, my mom's Christmas tree is plugged in and there's not another outlet nearby.

Me: *spikes eggnog*

Ummm . . . TMI?

I'm always amused by students whose default response to personal accountability is more flight than fight. Often, they resort to shock value in an effort to distract us from the actual issue. Fortunately, it takes a lot to make me squirm, so I'm ready for just about anything.

Me: I see you haven't logged into your classes in over a week. What's up?

Student, immediately defensive: I have my period and if you don't believe me, ask my mother.

Me: Okay, but how has your period prevented you from logging into your classes for an entire week?

Student: *You ever had cramps before?!*

Me: *launches into story about the day I got my first period*

Hey, if you can't beat 'em, join 'em!

New? Won't Do (the Work).

Another thing worth noting is the way a student handles adversity. I've found many of my virtual learners throw in the towel when they encounter what is typically their first stumbling block: finding and submitting their first assignment. In anticipation of new students' struggle with this, I created a document of written and visual instructions, complete with screenshots from the courses. Teach a man to fish and all that. Still, some refuse to even cast a line.

Student: I can't find the assignment; that's why I didn't do it.

Me: No worries! I've sent instructions that explain in words and in pictures where you'll find your assignment. Don't hesitate to let me know if you need anything at all!

Fifteen seconds later . . .

Student: I still can't do it. I don't know how.

Me: Those instructions I sent will really help!

Student: It's all new to me.

Me: Just because it's new doesn't mean you can't do it! You have to *try*! Have you looked at the instructions I sent?

Student: What instructions?

Hey, Mom, Can We Focus on Your Kid?

As many student issues as I've dealt with, they pale in comparison to the encounters I've had with parents. One would think adults understand children are priority, but sadly, that's not always the case.

Me: Hello! How are you today?

Parent: I'm sick.

Me: Oh, no! I'm sorry to hear that. You weren't feeling well the last time we spoke. I'm calling because—

Parent: *provides complete list of ailments, including graphic description of an enlarged colon*

Me: I, uh, am very sorry . . . to . . . hear . . . I'm actually calling to discuss your son's lack of progress in his online courses. Do you know he's exceptionally behind in every class? I've been trying to reach you for—

Parent: *continues to list ailments, apparently confusing me with a doctor*

Me: That sounds painful, I'm really very sorry you're not feeling well, so how 'bout those failing grades, eh? How can I better help your—

Parent: There's just no way I can get better if the doctor doesn't refill my prescription. I can't even drive because of these bunions. . . .

I honestly don't remember how that conversation ended. I think I blacked out.

Not My Kid!

On the opposite end of the Me! Me! Me! spectrum are the parents who are a wee bit too involved in their child's education. And by involved, I mean it's likely Dad is doing the work himself. No wonder they take feedback so personally!

9:45 p.m. email: I am livid my daughter was accused of cheating. Please respond to this message within the hour to rectify the situation so we can sleep tonight.

10:45 p.m. email: I see we won't be hearing from you this evening. It's a shame you don't care about the well-being of your students.

3:30 a.m. email: I *cannot sleep*. The whole day went downhill after receiving your message accusing my daughter of plagiarism. *lists reasons why his student couldn't have cheated*

7:30 a.m.: *my phone rings* The same email-sending parent leaves a three-minute voicemail repeating the content from his written messages, ending with a passive-aggressive shot: "Perhaps your supervisor can let me know if you're out of the office."

9:00 a.m.: *I return the parent's call and listen patiently as he talks at me, explaining that it's impossible his daughter has cheated and I am clearly wrong.*

9:15 a.m.: *I seize the opportunity to speak* Unfortunately, I have documents from our plagiarism-checker app that show exactly where on the web your daughter found the information. There's also a hyperlink to the website in her essay, so . . .

9:16 a.m.: *parent is silent*

9:17 a.m.: The good news is this is her first offense and we believe in students learning from their mistakes. She may resubmit under the following conditions . . .

9:20 a.m.: That'll be just fine. *hangs up*

Can We Just Dumb It Down?

Excerpt of actual phone call with a parent:

Parent: I don't think it's right my son has to take two English courses during his senior year.

Me: Unfortunately, he failed English last year, which is

why he's in the class again. We doubled up to keep him on track for graduation.

Parent: That just seems really unfair.

Me: Oh? I guess I thought it was helpful. Any chance he'd be able to recover the failed credits in summer school?

Parent: He's not going to school in the summer!

Me: Then, this really is our best bet. Doubling up means he'll graduate on time and won't have to work during the summer.

Parent: *sighs loudly in my ear* Fine, but can we just dumb it down a little? Like maybe he only has to do half of each class?

Me: *prays for strength*

What Up, Boo?
With all the truly frustrating situations I deal with, I appreciate the levity afforded by kids forgetting to shift into "student" mode in their emails. While there are certainly messages that can be construed as disrespectful and inappropriate, some are just plain fun!

Excerpt of student email:

Dear Mrs. J or other fam,
I have questions about stuff and was hoping someone would be able to call me. Or maybe y'all are robots?
Thanks, boo.
[Signed, Student]

Excerpt of my response:

What's shakin', bacon!
My robot has the day off, so I'd be happy to give you a
ring-a-ding-ding whenever you're ready to chat. Lemme
know what time works best for you.
Your boo,
Mrs. J

Say Hello to My Little Friend, the IP Address
When students enter my virtual classroom, they must log in and provide their name. It's not unusual for them to sign in with their initials rather than full names, so when necessary, we use their unique IP address to identify students and their whereabouts. When stuff like the following scenario happens, 'tis necessary to use that IP address:

Me: Welcome to class! Please type hello in the chat box if you can hear me.

Student A: Hello!

Student B: What's up?

Student C: Bitches ain't shit!

Student C continues to make it rain with cuss words, so I remove her from the classroom. Afterward, I call her to discuss her behavior and she, of course, vehemently denies it was her. Mom gets on the phone and supports her daughter's innocence, explaining she was sitting beside her the entire time. I am left no choice but to involve our tech team, which traces the IP address and confirms the vulgarity came from the student's personal computer.

Even with this proof, the student continues to deny it. I am instructed to give the family a warning and second chance; I do so and we move on.

The following week, a similar situation takes place in another teacher's classroom. We once again trace the IP address and conclude it's the same student. I am tasked with calling home a second time:

Me: *explains it happened again*

Mother: I'm sure my daughter doesn't even know those words!

Me: *rolls eyes to the back of my skull*

Before the student can be disciplined for the second offense, she commits a third in yet another teacher's classroom.

This time, our tech team traces the IP address to a local library and, per Google Maps, it's a few miles from where the student lives. Guess who gets to call home again!

Me: *explains what happened*

Mother: My daughter isn't even home! It couldn't be her!

Me: Any chance she's at the library?

Mother: *silence*

The student is withdrawn the next morning.

Bizarre excuses and lame cop-outs are hardly new developments in the world of education, but we've certainly come a long way from the ol' "the dog ate my homework" bit. No need to fear technology, though; teachers have embraced it and we're expertly using it to guide our detective work. My favorite example of a teacher combatting students' rampant cheating is one who created a fake webpage full of "answers" to her exams. She catfished her students and they fell for it!

To those who maintain the Internet is the devil (*waves to my mom*), I can appreciate your concerns. However, let's at least recognize the way technology also connects people across the globe, provides accessible learning to those who wouldn't otherwise have it and makes important advancements in every field from education to medicine. Since the beginning of time, students have made excuse after excuse for not doing their schoolwork; technology is hardly to blame. Until the day kids realize they're spending more time finding a work-around than doing the actual work, I don't foresee their excuse factory shutting down anytime soon. With or without technology, kids will be kids. And in the meantime, I will laugh at them and write about them for all of us to enjoy.

Now if you'll excuse me, my iPhone just hacked into my oven. Darn, guess I can't cook dinner tonight!

Teacher Truth

Having kids? Good luck naming them.

Baby-Naming Triggers, Classroom PTSD and Other Predicaments Only Teacher-Parents Will Understand

I realized it was happening during my first year of teaching. Since I started my job, I'd been fighting the urge to straighten lines of people at the movie theater and biting my tongue so I didn't correct the cashier's grammar at Target. The involuntary public shift from civilian to teacher mode was upon me, and although I tried, there was nothing I could do to stop it. Finally, one day in the grocery store, I broke.

One minute I was a normal shopper squeezing peaches; the next, I heard myself announcing, *"We do not run in the produce aisle!"* I couldn't control the volume or authoritative tone with which I corrected those unsuspecting kids that day—they might as well have been tardy students booking it down the hallway to class. They stopped in their tracks, heads turned in the direction of my misplaced teacher voice, and I had no choice but to own it. "What if you fall? Or run into me and I drop these perfect peaches!" I cautioned with a friendly, don't-eff-with-me smile. It wasn't surprising to see most people back their grocery-laden carts away from me, but I took special notice of those who made eye contact as a show of solidarity.

My people, I whispered to myself.

Since that day, I am forever incapable of taking off my teacher hat and returning to the blissful oblivion the average person enjoys on a daily basis. I jump into action whenever I see a need to wrangle chaos and automatically call out anything or anyone I sense as an impending hazard. My metamorphosis was largely unexpected and remains strictly unintentional; it's as though my school day never ends, it and all its procedural stuffs are now permanently engrained in me. I hate to admit it, but I am no longer capable of functioning like an ordinary contributing member of society.

Then I became a parent, and this train really went off its tracks.

It began with attempts to name our baby. As anyone who works with children can attest, our feelings about those kids stay with us long after they've moved on. In the best-case scenarios, their names bring back fond memories of quirky personality traits and fantastic work ethics. In the not-so-best scenarios, a mere mention of their name has us curled into the fetal position under a table. These latter connotations are what make the already daunting task of naming a human being even more problematic for educators.

My husband and I are *both* teachers, which complicated things further for us. He loved the name Isaac, but because an Isaac sat in the second row of my seventh-period class and made my life a living hell, Isaac was no longer an option. No matter how hard I vied for a Mia, my husband couldn't shake the recollection of Mia's overbearing parents circa 2004 and vetoed hard. Couple this teacher–parent dilemma with the last name Jankowski and the struggle is so real you can taste it.

When all was said and done, there were exactly two baby names we agreed on, one for each gender. We didn't know if we were having a boy or girl, and because we understood our already tiny list o' names could be ruined at any moment by a new student or happenstance encounter in the cafeteria, I was thankful for a late July due date since it allowed me to avoid all students during the last months of my pregnancy. Because that's normal. We welcomed a baby boy and named him Brady, in case you're in a similar predicament. You're welcome.

As a teacher, I put a lot of pressure on myself to raise my baby "right." I didn't exactly know what that looked like yet, but when Brady was about a month old, I felt compelled to mold him into the kind of kid who enjoyed learning as much as he enjoyed shitting up his back. On some level, I believed my success as an educator was indicative of my success as a mother, which doesn't even make sense because every parent knows it takes at least eighteen years to determine if we've raised an empathetic, hardworking individual or a Cheetos-eating sponge who lives in our basement. My anxieties about being a teacher–parent manifested into the need to control every aspect of Brady's early development. I was the conductor; he was my orchestra of properly achieved milestones.

Baby Einstein videos were the backdrop of his childhood because I fell for the hype, and I made sure to narrate even the most mundane of activities to hone his language skills. "Look, Brady! Mommy's on the verge of a nervous breakdown! *B* is for *breakdown!*"

When the day came to choose a preschool, I sufficiently overwhelmed myself with spreadsheets of a dozen schools, analyzing every detail down to the kinds and quantities of their snack offerings. After weeks of deliberation, I finally settled on the most "academic" of the toddler programs and scheduled a visit to the school. As an educator already comfortable correcting perfect strangers, I was now also inexplicably convinced everyone who interacted with my child needed—nay, *wanted!*—my input.

Input is the word people use when they don't realize they're being obnoxious.

I introduced myself to the preschool staff like, "Hello, I'm a teacher and a parent, ipso facto, an expert in all the things. Please hold my jacket while I share my brilliant thoughts for updating your curriculum." I imagine they were pretty happy when Brady graduated to kindergarten.

Without realizing it, I was turning into the very thing I tried avoiding in my classroom: the parent who moves heaven and earth to protect her child from adversity, aka the lawnmower parent.

Lawnmower parents strive to save their children from all hardship and challenge lest they experience the dreaded F-word: *failure*! Some lawnmowers have an underhanded agenda and a parenting style that can best be described as *balls-out, no-holds-barred, plotting every point of a kid's education because the stakes are too high to leave anything to chance.* These are the moms and dads who interfere with every aspect of their child's education. From handpicking every teacher to disputing every point on a test, lawnmower parents rarely let their kids do their own academic bidding.

A lot of us, though, are well intentioned and just want the best for our children. It's just that we don't always see the value in the struggle. That was me. I believed I was doing right by my child, and as a teacher, I'm privy to the behind-the-scenes goings-on of education, which is exactly *why* I felt it necessary to do a little lawn-mowing.

If you thought my preschool pursuits were insane, you should've seen me when it came time to traverse the terrain of kindergarten.

I've known elementary teachers who held informal drafts to determine who gets which incoming kindergarten students, specifically boys with late summer birthdays. Stop me if you've heard this one, but little boys tend to have a more difficult time acclimating to the structure of a school day. That's a nice way of saying they're high freaking maintenance. Teachers try to separate these crazy little nuggets as to distribute the load equally among themselves. So, what did I do when my crazy nugget and his July 26 birthday were headed to kindergarten?

Naturally, I vetted his teachers like the government running background checks on the potential secretary of Homeland Security candidates. I interviewed parents, kids and other teachers, determined to find the teacher who ruled her class-room with a stern yet fair hand, gave hugs and not too much candy and focused heavily on phonemic awareness. I, of course, also engaged in serious social media reconnaissance.

There was no shame in my lawn-mowing game.

Fast-forward to when I first met my son's would-be principal, whereupon I handed him a typed letter requesting the teacher I'd finally decided deserved the honor of educat-ing my blue-eyed angel. I justified my actions, citing "the utmost importance of this formidable year." *We must build a strong foundation now! Everything depends upon this year! Kindergarten is do-or-die!* Every night around two a.m., my neurosis reminded me elementary school was a larger stage on which my parenting would be critiqued. As we were now officially enrolled in the school district where we planned to remain for the next twelve years, I took great care to make sure my sweet Brady's first year was successful. Which is to say, I lawn-mowed the shit out of kindergarten.

Because I know teachers judge students by the company they keep, I endeavored to handpick my son's playmates to ensure the company he kept wouldn't have him smoking meth in the little boys' room. Gone were planned playdates and day drinking with other moms of my choice; now my precious firstborn would be subjected to all rungs on the social ladder. Most teacher–parents will openly deny, yet secretly believe, that our kids' friends have to meet the following completely reasonable, totally fair criteria before we approve of them. A potential pal must . . .

- Get good grades
- Behave in class
- Be active in clubs or sports
- Have parents who limit screen time; read to him for 40 minutes every day; instill good manners; feed him only organic, locally sourced food; and shower him with positive praise as to build his self-confidence, thereby making him a good influence on others

Jesus, take the wheel.

Because clearly I'm a fair person, I held my own kid to a set of equally delusional standards. I think most parents tend to be harder on their firstborn, and my husband and I were no different. Except we were both teachers at local schools, and in a small town like ours, that meant we were already under the scrutiny of the public eye. In turn, we doubled down, determined to raise a conscientious, respectful kid and not a big douchebag who would rain down shame on the family name.

We were especially hard on Brady when it came to academics, but it was for his own good since he was a child prodigy and all. During our first parent-teacher conference on the parent side, my husband inquired about the rigors of kindergarten math, and I asked when the class would start reading chapter books. The teacher smiled and blinked at us.

To this day, I appreciate the professional courtesy (and Herculean strength) she showed by waiting to laugh at us until we were gone.

Brady's only saving grace was his two younger sisters. They were close in age and required much of my time and energy, which worked well because, as it turned out, I needed to spend considerably less time and energy on Brady. Through a bit of trial and error, I realized I was doing my children exactly no favors customizing their experiences to match the vision of success I had in my head. Also, with Brady as my guinea pig, I learned I wasn't so terrible at the whole parenting thing. That boost in confidence allowed me to trust my instincts and stop second-guessing the other educators my children came in contact with. And you know what's crazy? Being a high school English teacher *and* a mom didn't make me an expert in all things teaching. Weird, right?

By the time all three of my kiddos were in school, I'd reeled in my teacher–parent paranoia just enough to pass for one of those normal moms. My kids are happier and more well adjusted now that they're making their own friends *and* mistakes, and I'm significantly less stressed having relinquished academic control to their teachers, who turned out to be fantastic. I now recognize where I am of value (volunteering to read to the class) and where I am not (offering to tidy up another teacher's desk), but that doesn't mean I've stopped encouraging discussions to assess the validity of a standards-based report card.

I am only human, after all.

Stuff I Didn't Expect to Miss about Traditional Teaching

I didn't have my own classroom at my last brick-and-mortar job. Considered a "traveling teacher," I had to rotate between different colleagues' rooms when they were empty. I hated every second of the dashing to and from; there was no time for my pregnant self to pee, and by the time I got to the next class, I was sweating profusely. I also didn't like sharing; it felt like nothing was truly mine. One of my colleagues actually counted his pencils after I had a class in his room and would come looking for me at the end of the day if any were missing.

I'm not kidding.

When I considered leaving that school in favor of a work-from-home opportunity, I felt a little guilty because I'd just finished an Advanced Placement Literature and Composition curriculum and was excited to teach it. I obviously didn't feel guilty enough, though, because I sure did throw my deuces up and never look back. Smell ya later, traditional classrooms that weren't even mine and the crazy pencil-counting mofos in them!

I count my blessings every day that I'm able to work from home, though I am surprised by some of the things I miss about face-to-face teaching. Dude and his prized pencil collection? I actually miss him! That kind of lunacy makes for good giggles over half-priced appetizers at happy hour, but my current colleagues don't even live in my state, so there goes that. I'm also lamenting my old wardrobe, especially the shoes. I had a pair for every day of the month, you guys! My shoe game was strong, my feet, as they say, were *on fleek*.

I mean, I think they still say *on fleek*? I wouldn't know because I'm not as exposed to current slang as I used to be. Strangely, I miss that, too.

These days, I talk to my dog more than to people and my rockin' shoe collection has been replaced by slippers. Don't get me wrong, I'm not complaining; I'm totally fine "going to work" in pajama pants. It's just that I never expected to miss these things, and I want you to know if you're still in the traditional trenches, you shouldn't take this stuff for granted.

Face-to-Face Conversations

I like to watch a person physically react while we communicate, and that's rarely possible in my current position. The majority of my daily conversations are now via phone or email. I miss seeing a student's face light up when a concept suddenly clicks! I long for the silent conversations that take place with just one glance at a colleague. And I miss the hell out of rolling my eyes with my team-teacher when our drunk-on-power school board member walks down the hall. There's absolutely something to be said for these kinds of relationships; no artificial intelligence will ever replace human interactions.

Separation of Roles

Working from home blurs the line between work and life responsibilities. If I'm not sorting testing data, I'm sorting socks. If I'm not on the phone with students, I'm on the phone with our pediatrician asking about my five-year-old's rash. I used to try to do all the things at the same time, but the now-infamous Toilet Call taught me a valuable lesson. Let's just say I didn't realize my webcam was on, okay? My best efforts to wear one hat at a time have been gravely unsuccessful, though I'm still grateful to be able to do it all from the comfort of my own home. I wish I could say "privacy of my own home," but privacy went out the window after that Toilet Call. . . .

A Sense of Community

I basically force my colleagues to be my friends by regularly showing up in their inboxes with pictures of my kids or oversharing details of the Toilet Call in our instant message chats. This helps recapture a small part of the traditional sense of community I was spoiled with in my brick and mortar, but there's just no replacing the coworker who bursts through your classroom door like *Seinfeld*'s Kramer with the next *greatest idea ever.* The regular collaboration, bumping into one another in the hallway and sharing inside jokes over lunch are just a few of the things that can't be replicated.

People Believing I Have a Job
I suffer from 1950s throwback syndrome, whereby my contributions are invisible and unappreciated because, like my maternal predecessors, I hold down the fort within the confines of my home. Because I do not leave my house, nor do I wear pants with zippers, everyone finds it really hard to believe that I somehow earn a paycheck.

Insta-inspiration
Quick conversations in between classes or catching a quick peek of fellow teachers in their element have a way of inspiring us when we least expect it. It's those surprise moments, those quick boosts, that make me teary for my brick-and-mortar days. Very little in the virtual environment happens spontaneously; from scheduling meetings to accommodating multiple time zones to planning everything *twice* (always gotta be prepared for technical glitches), next to nothing is left to happenstance.

Janitors
Can I still say janitors? I mean no disrespect, especially because I miss these individuals more than most of the other people I used to work with. These sweet, sweet men and women would sweep my floors, clean my boards, arrange the classroom

furniture. They cleaned up vomit and spills and garbage, and they almost always had this dry sense of humor that you found either offensive or hilarious. I miss it all so much.

Getting to Know Families

I've actually gone an entire school year without ever speaking to some of my virtual students' parents! It wasn't for lack of trying, but when given the choice of whether or not to answer the phone, some choose to decline the call every time. Building a positive rapport with families is such an integral part of the student's success. I miss having moms and dads show up for conferences or visit my classroom to deliver their homemade Christmas cookies. Maybe I just miss the cookies?

Personal Pride in My Appearance

It's noon; have I brushed my teeth? Your guess is as good as mine.

Having My Finger on the Pulse

I miss waiting in the hall to greet my students. I used to do a lot of eavesdropping out there. I was a supersleuth on cafeteria duty, too, latching on to any detail relevant to my students' personal or academic well-being. As it stands now, I don't even know what music is pumping through my students' earbuds; in the traditional school setting, I would simply ask to have a listen. Students' personal lives and pop culture impact their education, and in my current position, I feel a stinging disconnect from both. Some of you may read that and think, "That's exactly the disconnect I want!" but proceed with caution: You just might miss that stuff if it's gone.

I won't lie: I do wonder if I'm as effective of an educator as I used to be, when I was physically experiencing the learning process with my students. If you're considering making the move from a brick and mortar to virtual, promise me you'll make sure you're moving for the right reasons. I know there's probably plenty about your school that makes you want to jump ship, or maybe you're like me and looking for a change that'll benefit your family. All I ask is that you weigh your pros and cons and learn something from my professional journey. Now that my kids are older and I don't have to schedule my life around their diaper blowouts or naps, the things I miss about my traditional teaching job have been on my mind a lot. Maybe it's just true that we always want what we can't have, but it's equally true that we never appreciate what we've got until it's gone.

Teaching Empathy

I wrote this essay the very afternoon I sat in a high school auditorium listening to Ms. Shulamit Bastacky's story of survival. Separated from her parents shortly after she was born, Shulamit spent the first years of her life in a dark basement with little nourishment and even less exposure to the outside world. Shulamit was one of the Holocaust's "Hidden Children," alive today only because a Roman Catholic nun risked her own life to save a Jewish infant's. While she was in that basement, entire generations of Shulamit's family were marked for death and slaughtered because of their ethnicity.

Yet I listened as Shulamit used words like *kindness* and *lucky* over and over as she recounted her experience.

After she had lived through such horrifying circumstances, the likes none of us will ever know, Shulamit's message of kindness and respect rises up like a phoenix. Even after October 27, 2018, when a lunatic with a gun and an anti-Semitic agenda killed eleven Jews at the Tree of Life synagogue in her hometown of Pittsburgh, Shulamit still manages to preach tolerance and acceptance.

If a woman who has looked the depths of evil square in the eye can find it within her heart to celebrate all the good this world has to offer, we need to pay attention to what she's saying. It is absolutely imperative that we educators bear witness to Shulamit's story and other examples of horrendous hate. Why? Because advocating and educating go hand in hand.

You don't think it's necessary? You don't think it's "our place"? Consider the following scenario that played out at a public high school a few miles from where I live:

Teachers walking into school are greeted by a man yelling, "To hell with you all Islam teachers!" He spews vitriol and threatens to sue the school and the teacher who assigned students to read *I Am Malala: The Girl Who Stood Up for Education and Was Shot by the Taliban*. The man brags that he has burned the book (which, incidentally, the school owned, so . . .) and posted it on social media. And if you ask him why, he'll tell you it's all in the name of Christianity. Oh, and fun fact: This happened in January 2019.

Don't tell me teaching empathy isn't necessary, and don't you dare say it's not our job.

I used to work in a district where biracial students would only claim their white ancestry. The refusal to acknowledge their multiethnic background confused me, especially since I had come from a school where people of color were proud of their heritage. Then, I met the mayor of their small town and overheard him telling a racist joke. I suddenly saw things through my students' eyes. Diversity wasn't celebrated there;

it was disrespected. On a separate occasion in that same district, one of my students declared she was a lesbian. Of course, she yelled this in the middle of class because why wait for an appropriate time? Ahhh, teenagers. Anyway, I paused from the lesson, responded, "As long as you're happy and respectful, you can be whatever you want," then made a mental note to talk to her later. When we finally had the chance to chat, she confessed her outburst was meant to make another student feel bad, a student who wouldn't date her. Apparently, this boy had confided in her that he believed he was gay. Instead of supporting him, she humiliated him. I think there was something in the water that turned out more assholes per square mile than in neighboring towns. Once I was aware of the emotional complexity of the situation, I spoke with both students and learned kids had been bullying the boy who believed he was gay. Homosexuality wasn't tolerated in that district.

Before working there, I'd not been privy to the extensive bigotry and lack of compassion in the school and, apparently, the community. Everything looked so pristine from the outside; clean, manicured, well kept. But the insides were so ugly. I knew then that my students needed a lesson in empathy, and who better to give it than their teacher? My idea was met with some administrative pushback, but I persisted, and was eventually given permission under one condition: The project presentations must be open for the parents to attend . . . and criticize. I wasn't afraid of the repercussions of doing the lesson; I was more afraid of the repercussions of *not* doing it. We got to work.

Piggybacking off a research project I'd done in my previous school, the R.I.G.H.T.S. Project, I introduced my students to the importance of Recognizing Individuals of Global Humanity for a Tolerant Society. The major themes of the project, recognizing examples of human rights violations and learning how to foster tolerance through activism, seemed especially relevant to my particular community of learners. Despite the fact that most of the research topics were historical events such as the Armenian genocide, apartheid or Matthew Shephard's story, I made sure to draw comparisons to current examples of intolerance and bigotry. We focused on action items and discussed the ways we can combat things like racism, homophobia, sexism and other rights violations. Overtly, my goal was to have them bear witness to the stories of people who didn't look like them. Quietly, I was sending unspoken messages like, hey, the mayor of your town is a racist dick and here are intelligent ways to respond.

We pulled inspiration for our activism from the pages of Elie Wiesel's *Night* and Harper Lee's *To Kill a Mockingbird*. As was the case for way too many of those kids, the R.I.G.H.T.S. Project was the first time they'd ever been asked to learn about a topic they didn't necessarily agree with.

As per administration's requirements, we presented the projects at school one evening. Surrounded by parents and that gem of a mayor, I watched as students vehemently called for more understanding, compassion and tolerance from their school and their community. Some students bravely shared their personal experiences with racism and classism in front of the same people who had violated their rights. If that's not courage for a kid, I don't know what is. I believe our project provided a new lens through which students should respectfully view one another, but I also think those who needed it most learned to respect themselves a little more. Focusing on people and stories that were similar to their experiences made them feel worthy and valuable. I can't say for sure whether our time together changed their opinions or perspectives for the rest of their lives, but I felt good about showing them what exists beyond the confines of their small town and, in some cases, small minds.

But our work is far from over, fellow educators. We must commit ourselves to teaching tolerance and compassion and respect. The inspiration for action is right in front of us! Think of all the wonderful ways our students represent the world's differences: They're from diverse races, religions and ethnicities. They're part of the LGBTQ community. They hail from various socioeconomic backgrounds. All their different experiences color their young perspective and whatever that perspective is, they deserve to recognize themselves on the pages of our books, too. Shulamit says our goal should be to combine what's in our heads and hearts and use our energy for good, so let's combine education and empathy and make the world a better, safer, more loving place one lesson plan at a time.

In addition to using inclusive language and pronouns, the following are three other great ways to facilitate inclusiveness and tolerance into our classrooms. I've included ideas for varying age groups, because none of us are off the hook.

Inclusive Book Lists

Most of the stories I read when I was in school, including those in my history books, featured heroes that all looked the same: a bunch of white guys. Fortunately, many of today's books are evolving to include more diverse characters. The following titles certainly aren't all-encompassing—do you know how hard it was for a book nerd like me to narrow these down to just a few?!—but they're a great start. You know your students best, and I encourage you to find other titles that meet their needs, if necessary. Representation matters, which is why more inclusive reading needs to be part of our classrooms and pronto.

Preschool & Kindergarten

These titles celebrate our differences by encouraging self-acceptance and unlikely friendships and by breaking down stereotypes in a way even the youngest of readers can understand.

A Bad Case of Stripes, by David Shannon

Be Who You Are, by Todd Parr

Pink Is for Boys, by Robb Pearlman

Same, Same but Different, by Jenny Sue Kostecki-Shaw

The Skin You Live In, by Michael Tyler

Elementary School (grades 1–5)

Continuing the same themes as above, these books also dive a bit deeper into such topics as equality, acceptance and pride.

I'm Mixed!, by Maggy Williams

Introducing Teddy: A Gentle Story about Gender and Friendship, by Jessica Walton

Last Stop on Market Street, by Matt de la Peña

Pride: The Story of Harvey Milk and the Rainbow Flag, by Rob Sanders

Rickshaw Girl, by Mitali Perkins

Middle School (grades 6–8)

Written for kids who are at the age of importance (self-importance, that is), the following titles do a great job of introducing the idea of activism. Through poetry and historically accurate narratives, young adult readers confront such issues as racism and classism while learning how to advocate for what's right.

Can I Touch Your Hair?: Poems of Race, Mistakes, and Friendship, by Irene Latham and Charles Walters

Esperanza Rising, by Pam Muñoz Ryan

Front Desk, by Kelly Yang (suitable reading for younger grades, but great examples of activism older readers can emulate)

Irena's Children: Young Reader's Edition; A True Story of Courage, by Tilar J. Mazzeo, adapted by Mary Cronk Farrell

Red Scarf Girl: A Memoir of the Cultural Revolution, by Ji-li Jiang

High School (grades 9–12)

Timely and ultimately uplifting, these stories are great conversation starters for discussing topics such as prejudice and injustice, empowerment and self-worth, mental illness, education and so much more.

The 57 Bus: A True Story of Two Teenagers and the Crime That Changed Their Lives, by Dashka Slater

The Art of Being Normal, by Lisa Williamson

The Dangerous Art of Blending In, by Angelo Surmelis

I Am Malala: The Girl Who Stood Up for Education and Was Shot by the Taliban, by Malala Yousafzai

I Am Not Your Perfect Mexican Daughter, by Erika L. Sánchez

Love, Hate and Other Filters, by Samira Ahmed

Piecing Me Together, by Renée Watson

To●thpaste Activity

This activity is best suited for our beloved tweens (lookin' at you, middle school), but because the visual is so powerful, younger students will understand it as well. The objective is to remind students to use their words for good, to speak kindly. As a class, create a list of hurtful words (school-appropriate, of course—don't get fired and then blame me) that students have been called or have called others. Each time a new word is added to the list, squeeze out a bit of toothpaste, creating a clear correlation between hurtful words and the toothpaste. At the end of the activity, challenge a student to put all the toothpaste back into the tube. As he struggles and ultimately fails, emphasize this simple yet poignant fact: Once we say or post something hurtful, it's out there for good.

R.I.G.H.T.S. Project

I'm proud to share this amazing high school cross-curricular project, especially because Ms. Beth Ryce, my former colleague/ current dear friend who is arguably one of the most inspirational educators I know, created it. She'll tell you I helped, but this is truly her brainchild. We found the project lends itself perfectly to English and history classes but encourage you to involve every discipline. Make this bad boy truly interdisciplinary and then shut down your whole school for an afternoon and let all the students learn from one another. I don't want to brag (yes, I do), but the first year we did this, we turned it into a school-wide event and our local newspaper covered it and we invited a Holocaust survivor to speak to our students, and it was all kinds of amazing. I challenge you to top us (and then totally tell me about it because *yay* teamwork!).

You can download the complete lesson plan on my blog, WhenCrazyMeetsExhaustion.com, for use in your classroom, and Beth and I hope you do. Seriously. Do it. *stares at you until you're visibly uncomfortable*

The educational term *inclusion* initially referred to efforts to meet the learning needs of all our students, but I think it's time we revise the definition. I haven't asked her, but I'm pretty sure Shulamit would agree that for our classrooms to sincerely be "inclusive," we must acknowledge and respect our differences. Every child should feel represented and supported, and, yes, it is a teacher's responsibility to ensure this happens.

Sharing Is Caring: Resources Section

I hand-selected . . . (How else does a person select things? With their toes?) Aaaanyway, I've specifically chosen the following resources because they strike a balance between helpful and hilarious. You'll use some of them to write project-based lesson plans or learn about the latest educational technology, while others are good for giggles and shows of solidarity. Enjoy and good luck!

Yours in education,
Steph

- BadAssTeacher.org (supporting public schools + having the hard conversation = love)
- BoredTeachers.com (their memes are everything)
- Edutopia.org (established by visionary filmmaker George Lucas, who just might be education's best friend)
- Gerry Brooks's YouTube channel (you're welcome)
- TeachersPayTeachers.com (because why reinvent the wheel?)
- TED-Ed, ed.ted.com (TED's education offshoot and a fabulous resource for teachers and students)
- WeAreTeachers.com (I'm partial, what can I say? Check them out on Facebook and Instagram, too!)
- R.I.G.H.T.S Project on WhenCrazyMeetsExhaustion.com

Acknowledgments

I'm incredibly humbled anyone would spend their hard-earned money on my words. Would it be a cliché if I said this is a dream come true? Then I won't. But I will say THANK YOU.

My VHS family: The first, the best, always my favorite. I'll love you forever and a day.

My collaborative community, a fancy name for the brilliant educators who never flinched when I bombarded them for brainstorming help, made this book possible. I appreciate you all, especially Beth, Jen, Trish and my WhenCrazyMeets Exhaustion pals. XO.

To my husband, Zach, aka #HusbandWTF: Even though you'd interrupt my writing with a YouTube video about caulking baseboards or something, I couldn't have pulled this off without your support and patience. You make everything better. I really like you.

To the kids I birthed: Brady, Ella and Lyla, thank you for maintaining a general lack of interest in this book. You remind me where I belong . . . apparently in the kitchen making you another snack. I love you to pieces. Don't forget: Now we sell Mommy's book to all your teachers!

To the kids I taught: You've shaped my journey more than you know, and for that I am eternally grateful. Wishing the very best for you, always.

Mom, Dad and Michael: Thank you for your support and enthusiasm and help and love. We've come a long way from the third-grade Spelling Bee, eh? M-E-D-I-C-I-N-E.

Jenna and the Page Street Publishing team: This whole experience truly is the stuff of a little girl's dreams. You guys took a chance on me and no words can ever express my sincerest gratitude. I appreciate every comma, every email, every pep talk, every time you wanted to muzzle me but didn't. I'm hugging you. Can you feel it?

To the hard stuff: Even though you sting, I've noticed when we don't back down from you, amazing things happen. I pray more and more educators willingly embrace you because that's the only way we're going to get things done.

About the Author

English teacher by trade, smack-talker by nature, Stephanie Jankowski lives by the mantra, "Life is too short, laugh!" After she had three babies and replaced her classroom with a computer, Steph wanted an outlet to share/cope with/laugh at her personal and professional evolution. She started her humor blog WhenCrazyMeetsExhaustion in 2011, and its success earned her spots in bestselling humor anthologies, a beloved gig as director of the live-reading show Listen to Your Mother Pittsburgh, and an invitation to the White House, where she and other like-minded parents and educators shared an afternoon with former First Lady Michelle Obama.

Her blog has also gifted the opportunity to marry her first true loves, humor and education. Steph is a contributor to various educational companies and sites, including We Are Teachers. This is her first book, and writing it gave her the nervous poops.

For more of Stephanie's irreverent thoughts on education and parenting, check out her blog at WhenCrazyMeets Exhaustion.com. Or don't. She's not everyone's cup of tea and that's okay.